THE 2 IN 1 LIFE COACHING VALUE COLLECTION:

THE #1 ULTIMATE GUIDE HOW TO MASTER LIFE COACHING AND BUSINESS COACHING FOR BEGINNERS

ELVIN COACHES

© Copyright 2020 - **All rights reserved.**

The content contained within this book may not be reproduced, duplicated or transmitted without direct written permission from the author or the publisher.

Under no circumstances will any blame or legal responsibility be held against the publisher, or author, for any damages, reparation, or monetary loss due to the information contained within this book, either directly or indirectly.

Legal Notice:

This book is copyright protected. It is only for personal use. You cannot amend, distribute, sell, use, quote or paraphrase any part, or the content within this book, without the consent of the author or publisher.

Disclaimer Notice:

Please note the information contained within this document is for educational and entertainment purposes only. All effort has been executed to present accurate, up to date, reliable, complete information. No warranties of any kind are declared or implied. Readers acknowledge that the author is not engaged in the rendering of legal, financial, medical or professional advice. The content within this book has been derived from various sources. Please consult a licensed professional before attempting any techniques outlined in this book.

By reading this document, the reader agrees that under no circumstances is the author responsible for any losses, direct or indirect, that are incurred as a result of the use of the information contained within this document, including, but not limited to, errors, omissions, or inaccuracies.

CONTENTS

DON'T MAKE ME USE MY LIFE COACH VOICE

Introduction	9
1. THE ESSENCE OF ENLIGHTENED COACHING	15
Famous People Who Love Life Coaches	18
So, What Can a Life Coach Do for You?	20
Common Misconceptions of Life Coaches	26
Why You Should Become a Life Coach	29
Common Challenges of Life Coaching	32
Keeping It Private	34
2. THE INTUITIVE COACH	35
Benefits of Working With an Intuitive Life Coach	37
Methods of an Intuitive Life Coach	39
Law of Attraction	42
3. POWERFUL COACHING TECHNIQUES AND SKILLS	46
The Techniques You Need for Great Coaching	48
Techniques That Will Benefit Your Clients	49
4. THE TIME TRAVEL COACHING TECHNIQUE	57
Techniques to Create More Impact	62
Techniques Requiring More Skill	69
Other Effective Techniques	71
5. TYPES OF COACHING STYLES	73
The Coaching Approach	74

6. CHAPTER 5: GREAT QUESTIONS TO ASK 85
   WHEN COACHING SOMEONE
   Making a Transformation 86
   Open-Ended Questions 91
   More Tips for Asking the Appropriate 92
   Questions
   Some More Questions 95

7. THE SCIENCE OF HABITS 99
   Habits and Their Formation 100
   When You're Finally Ready to Make a Change 109
   What's in a Day? Or 21? 117
   How a Life Coach Can Help With Habit Change 118
   Promoting a Habit Challenge 120

8. THE MINDSET COACHING 121
   You Are Here to Do Extraordinary Things 123
   Who Can Use a Mindset Coach? 126
   How Does a Mindset Coach Help? 128
   The End of a Session 133

9. BUSINESS COACHING 135
   You as a Business Coach 138
   Selling Yourself as a Business Coach 140
   The Biggest Obstacles for Successful Business 143
   Coaching
   Building Trust 148

   Conclusion 153
   References 159

WHO WANTS TO BE A SUPERHERO IF YOU CAN BE A BUSINESS COACH?

Introduction 171

1. BUSINESS COACHING ON THE HIGHEST LEVEL — 177
   - What Can a Coach Really Do? — 181
   - Why You'll Love Being a Business Coach — 187
   - How to Become a Business Coach — 190

2. THE ESSENCE OF BUSINESS COACHING CREDIBILITY — 200
   - How to Build Credibility — 202
   - What to Avoid as a Coach — 208
   - Why Vulnerability is Important — 212
   - Help Your Client Become Vulnerable — 217
   - The Importance of Privacy — 221

3. TIME MANAGEMENT TIPS TO INCREASE PRODUCTIVITY — 222
   - Time Management Coach Strategies — 223
   - Why Procrastination is Bad — 228
   - How to Build a Habit — 232
   - Time in Terms of Philosophy — 236
   - Manage Your Time — 238
   - Who Are Your Prospective Clients? — 243
   - Steps to Increase Productivity — 246

4. MARKETING COACHING — 249
   - Who Is a Marketing Coach? — 250
   - Why Do Businesses Hire a Marketing Coach? — 254
   - Specific Marketing Strategies — 258
   - Complementing With a Blog — 261

5. COMMON BUSINESS COACHING QUESTIONS — 265
   - Dissecting the Grow Model — 267
   - Questioning Techniques — 274

6. TOP CORE BUSINESS COACHING SKILLS	280
Coaching Skills	281
Increasing Empathy	294
7. LEADERSHIP DEVELOPMENT COACH	298
Leadership Development Coaching	300
Benefits of Leadership Development Coaching	301
Skills Needed for Leadership Development Coaching	303
Principles of Leadership Development Coaching	307
Why Hire a Leadership Development Coach	309
Business/Life Balance	310
Conclusion	315
References	323

DON'T MAKE ME USE MY LIFE COACH VOICE

THE ART AND SCIENCE OF LIFE COACHING FOR NEWCOMERS

Just for you!

Scan the QR code to subscribe or follow the link
https://elvinlifecoaches.activehosted.com/f/3

A FREE GIFT TO OUR READERS

You're going to receive the

Wheel of Life Coaching Technique

and other goodies

INTRODUCTION

"The great thing in the world is not so much in where we stand as in what direction we are moving."

— OLIVER WENDELL HOLMES

Picture a man wandering aimlessly on the road. He is going in a certain direction, but if you were to stop and ask him where, he would not be able to tell you. This is because he has no actual direction and will just go where the road leads. The man will not know if he has arrived where he's supposed to be because he never really knew where he was going. When he's hungry, he will eat. When he's thirsty, he will drink. When he's tired, he will sleep. He will respond to his physiological needs, but beyond this, his life will have no real meaning. He is just doing what is needed to exist.

Unfortunately, this is a metaphor for how so many people live. People wander aimlessly through life with no real direction. They have no goals or ambitions, and therefore never create the life they were meant to have. I want better for you because I know that you deserve it. We all deserve to live a fulfilling life as long as we are willing to work for it. You must develop direction in order to truly get where you want to be. To have direction, you must create solid goals, objectives, and pathways for how you want to get there.

This can be challenging for those who are not used to it. Many individuals have learned to retreat when life gets challenging. They have numerous problems and have no idea how to resolve them. The great thing is, you have the answers inside of you. That's right! With any problems that come your way, you have the ability to come up with a solution. You have the capability, just like anyone else, to figure out your true path and create a life that you desire.

Sometimes, we just need some guidance from an outside source. The answers are somewhere inside of us, but we cannot figure out how to find them. There can be many reasons for this, like past failures, disappointments, pain, trauma, abuse, and a wealth of other setbacks. These act as mental roadblocks, and my goal is to help you tear them all down. We can make this happen together through the art of life coaching.

Life coaching is an interesting field. Many people confuse it with counseling, but the objectives are quite different. With counselors or therapists, their goal is to find solutions for you while dealing with mental health disorders, whereas a life coach helps you figure out things for yourself. They don't tell you how to live your life, but help you determine the type of life you want to live. A life coach will provide you with clarity so you can see the answers to your problems right in front of you. From there, it is up to you to move in the right direction.

By reading through the chapters in this book, you will learn about the immense benefits of life coaching and how to become one yourself so you can assist others in finding their pathway towards a better life too. By the time you are done, you will have a detailed understanding of what life coaching is and the immense benefits it provides. This book will also cover different types of life coaches that exist, the various techniques and methodologies used in coaching practices, how to form positive habits, and effectively coaching those who need it.

If you have been feeling lost and uncertain about life, don't be too hard on yourself. It happens to everybody, but the key is to find the right solutions. This is what I am here to help you with through my book, *Don't Make Me Use My Life Coach Voice*. I understand the feeling of being lost and in pain. I know how it feels to not know where you're going. These feelings are not unusual, so never think yourself to be weird for having them.

However, you also cannot allow yourself to live this way forever. At some point, you must look towards greener pastures to find and create better circumstances. Otherwise, you will be stuck in an existence that you find miserable and restrictive. Once again, you have the power to get out of your rut because you know yourself the best. I am simply here to guide you. If you are ready to start your life coaching journey, come with me and I will show you how.

(David, n.d.)

WHO AM I?

Well, before you take my advice, I assume you would like to know more about me first. I am part of a group called Elvin Coaches, which is a collective of people who love to help and guide others towards a better life and circumstances. We all met each other during an event in Bali, Indonesia several years ago.

We were there to study the life coaching process and bonded with one another almost instantly. Over the years, we have become closer and now feel like a family.

Life coaching has become a passion for all of us, and we have collectively helped numerous individuals during our many years of training. Life coaching is not just a career or business at Elvin Coaches, but a passion and lifestyle by which we all swear by. This means that if we are not actively helping people, we feel an emptiness inside, as if there's a piece of us missing.

Because we are so passionate about life coaching, we wanted to impart our knowledge and training to you. We felt that the best way to reach the masses was by writing a book detailing our ideas. We want to help you, the reader, learn about life coaching so you can benefit from the practice and even become a life coach yourself someday if you choose. The information provided in this book, *Don't Make Me Use My Life Coach Voice*, helped all of us during some of the most challenging times in our lives, and we are confident it will help you too, just like it has for many other clients that have crossed our paths.

All of us at Elvin Coaches still experience the ups and downs of life. There are days when we are on top of the world, while others, we are down and out and just want to hide somewhere. Getting through life is a constant battle, and none of us will ever tell you differently. We do not promise that all of your problems will go away; however, you will be equipped with better tools to handle them. After learning the techniques used in life coaching, you will look at your life in a completely different way.

Ultimately, we want to help you find the solutions for your life and also guide you into becoming life coaches yourself. Once you learn to put yourself back together, you can help other people do the same. That is the mindset here at Elvin Coaches. We coached ourselves to become better people. Now, we will help you become coaches in the same manner.

All of us at Elvin Coaches want to thank you in advance for listening to our words. If you are ready to become the ultimate life coach, keep reading.

Team

1

THE ESSENCE OF ENLIGHTENED COACHING

Enlightenment

For those of you who are sports fans, I want you to think about your favorite athlete. If you are not a sports fan, think about an actor, singer, or any type of performer that you admire. How do these individuals make you feel when you watch them perform at their highest level? I imagine that it's a powerful experience for you. Now, I want you to realize that all of these individuals had someone behind the scenes to help hone their craft and provide motivation. In most cases, it was some type of coach. All great performers out there had some assistance in becoming who they are with their talents. Athletes have head coaches, defensive coaches, or offensive coaches. Other celebrities may have voice coaches, acting coaches, or speech coaches.

After understanding this, does it make their talents seem any less significant? Of course, it doesn't because all great men and women had some type of guidance throughout their lives. It might have been direct face-to-face coaching or learning from afar. Either way, everybody needs help, and getting it does not make them any less smart, talented, or skilled.

Since these entertainers have coaches for their careers, why would someone not consider having a coach for their lives? A life coach is someone who will help you live your best life. They will be a guiding light so you can make the best decisions for yourself. The art of life coaching provides a synergistic relationship between the coach and their client. Eventually, this will lead a person to tap into their full potential and live the life they were meant to have. So often, people are just existing rather than living. They are constantly falling short of where their talents can actually take them. It's time to change this routine and give your life new meaning.

If you are feeling lost or need to be pointed in the right direction, a life coach will help you grow out of this by analyzing your current situation, identifying your limiting beliefs, and customizing a plan to help you overcome any obstacles standing in your way. They can help you see the big picture and focus your mind on your desired goals.

The relationship a person has with their life coach is personal and professional at the same time. A life coach will learn a lot about you, but will also need to keep boundaries. They cannot be manipulated by emotions, so they must remain objective. Still, the partnership can be creative by targeting the help towards individual wants and needs. No one person is the same, so a good coach is able to identify the best ways to help different clients which are unique to that individual. Through their assistance, a client will be able to:

- Create a clear vision for themselves based on their specific goals in life.
- Modify goals, as needed, based on changes in circumstances.
- Discover more about themselves.
- Confront their fears and dark past if they have one.
- Develop a plan of action with concrete strategies for change.

A combination of all of these will lead to a more fulfilling life. When you start working with a life coach, you will understand the true value it brings. If you act as a life coach for others, you will understand how helping others allows you to grow yourself.

FAMOUS PEOPLE WHO LOVE LIFE COACHES

While we don't want you to do something simply because a celebrity does, the fact that so many famous people in their field attribute their success to life coaches is a testament to how beneficial the practice can be. It has boosted some careers and revitalized others. The following are some celebrities who credit life coaches with helping them immensely during their careers (Casano, 2016).

- Oprah Winfrey: She credits much of her success to her personal life coach, Martha Beck, and has been a major advocate of this practice for decades. She even suggests life coaches to members of her audience who may be struggling.
- Nia Long: She has been an actress for over 20 years and credits her life coach for helping her live a more fulfilling life.
- Danny Bonaduce: After his success in the highly popular series *The Partridge Family,* Mr. Bonaduce suffered immensely due to drug use, homelessness, and legal issues. After working with a life coach, he was able to become grounded again and get his life back on track. He loved life coaching so much that he eventually became one himself.
- Von Miller: He is the star linebacker for the Denver Broncos football team. Back in 2011 and 2013, he had

problems with the law. His entire career could have been over. Luckily, this did not happen to Mr. Miller. He sought out a life coach to help him turn his life around and has since become a Super Bowl champion and MVP.
- Metallica: Arguably one of the most famous bands of all time. After going through some heated feuds, the members received help from a life coach and were able to realign themselves with a common goal. They worked together in harmony to achieve great success.
- Leonardo DiCaprio: He has worked with probably the most famous and successful life coach of all time, Tony Robbins. While Mr. DiCaprio is silent about the work he did with Mr. Robbins, his immense movie success speaks for itself.
- Chuck Liddell: A highly successful MMA fighter and UFC legend, Mr. Liddell is both physically and mentally tough. During his prime, he was one of the best and most feared fighters in the world. Mr. Liddell actually worked with Tony Robbins at one point to help him strengthen the mental aspect of his game. This would complement his physical gifts pretty well, making him a lean, mean, fighting machine.
- Hugh Jackman: Mr. Jackman also worked with Tony Robbins, whom he had been seeking out for years. The specifics are not well known, but Mr. Jackman has nothing but praise for Mr. Robbins.

- Andre Agassi: One of the greatest tennis players of all time, Mr. Agassi credits the help of a life coach for taking him from the 126th to the number one tennis player during his time.
- Serena Williams: Probably the greatest female tennis player of all time, Ms. Williams also credits Tony Robbins for helping her with the success she has had. After battling injuries for years, she was stressed and worn out. When she worked with Mr. Robbins, she was able to persist and train through her injuries and eventually win a Grand Slam.

This is a truly versatile list of people, which showcases the effectiveness of life coaching. The practice can always be targeted towards an individual's needs, making them the best version of who they are. If you still discount the value of a good life coach, keep on reading. Well, keep on reading regardless.

SO, WHAT CAN A LIFE COACH DO FOR YOU?

Essentially, a person will work with a life coach because they want to have a better life tomorrow than they have today. They want to see growth in every area of their lives, including personal, professional, health, and relationships. A life coach can help you identify the gaps that exist between where you are and where you want to be. Once this happens, it will be your job to build the bridges and close the gaps.

When you are wondering about the necessity of life coaching, you're impeding yourself from unlocking an extraordinary life. Even the most successful among us can improve in some way. There is always something missing that we cannot find unless someone guides us in doing so. Having the talent and bird's-eye view of a life coach can help all of us find what is holding us back.

Your relationship with a life coach does not have to be short term. They can help and guide you throughout your life and struggles. You might be wondering right now what the difference is between a life coach and a friend. Well, a friend will have a personal connection with you, so they will provide advice from an area of subjectivity rather than objectivity. Furthermore, while a friend can provide advice, a trained life coach can help uncover a person's deepest thoughts to determine their strengths and weaknesses, and how they can improve upon both. There are a few key elements that make working with a life coach worth it.

Accountability

Most life coaches have a long-term relationship with their clients, as long as the chemistry is there. They will also have regularly scheduled phone calls or in-person meetings to assess their clients' progress. Essentially, if you are not making positive changes in your life, you will have to answer for them. A good life coach will not allow you to make excuses. If a plan was laid for success, you better believe you will be held accountable for following it.

Think of this as having a personal trainer while you're working out. You will push yourself much harder when you know someone is watching you. This is just human nature. The same goes for having a life coach. When you know someone will follow up with you and expect results, then you are more likely to work harder to achieve them.

"Integrity is doing the right thing, even when no one is looking."

— C.S. LEWIS

The above quote relates to people just doing what they're supposed to, even if no one is watching them. Unfortunately, people become lackadaisical when they think they're alone and no one is holding them accountable. Even the mildest pressure of knowing a life coach will be asking some tough questions is motivation enough for people to get in gear.

Expertise

Life coaches are trained and skilled in knowing how to help you come up with the right goals, improve your financial success, and better structure your personal life. With a coach like this on your side, you can significantly increase your success. Remember, Michael Jordan had Phil Jackson; Tom Brady had Bill Belichick; and Mike Tyson, at his best, had Kevin Rooney. Even top business professionals have someone advising them. Behind every successful person throughout history is a coach of some kind guiding them to be their best.

Delivery

While your friends and family members might mean well, they do not always know the right things to say. Their words can turn into lecturing or nagging, which is not helpful at all. A well-trained life coach knows exactly how to motivate their clients so they can be at their very best. The motivational words of a life coach are usually provided over the phone or some type of video call, like Skype or Zoom. In-person meetings happen too, but if a life coach lives in another area and has multiple clients, remote access is the best option and one they will likely choose.

Speed of Progress

Clients who work with life coaches often report that everything in their lives starts moving at rapid speed and much more efficiently. Again, having accountability plays a huge role. People are pushed to make actual changes, which means life will be improving in many ways. Even during uncomfortable times, forward progress is happening. In fact, during times of discomfort, the most positive changes are happening.

People seek out life coaches because they feel their lives have no meaning. Even if they're successful in one aspect, they could be lacking in many others. A life coach can point out how simple some solutions are, and how minor changes can ultimately lead to major success. When you decide to go down this path, dreams that were once out of reach can become a reality. Immediately after working with a life coach, you will find yourself changing and growing in many of the following ways:

- Taking more effective action steps. Remember that just because you're acting does not mean you are moving in the right direction.
- Ignoring petty annoyances that disrupt your day.
- Creating momentum in your life to achieve great results. Success can be addictive once you get a taste of it.
- Setting more affirmative goals based on what you actually want in life. This is because your clarity and focus are much better, and you will be able to define a vision for success.
- Identifying your limiting beliefs that have been holding you back.

In addition to these, there are many personal adjustments that may occur based on the individual. Some of these changes include:

- Increased financial stability resulting from better money management, starting a business, getting a promotion, or a combination of many things.
- Being able to maintain a work/life balance. Understanding which one needs your attention and what moment becomes essential.
- Learning to communicate more succinctly and effectively. Wasting words will no longer be a problem for you.
- Fostering more powerful connections professionally and personally
- Achieving weight loss and/or fitness goals
- Managing an important life or business transition

There are many different types of life coaches, and we will describe them in more detail throughout the different chapters in this book. Some coaches focus on well being and spirituality. Others are more professionally minded and do things like helping you get organized or take a left brained approach to improving your life. You can seek out specific types of coaches based on what your particular needs are.

While life coaching does not require a specific certification, there are many training programs out there that will provide you with the tools and certifications to make you a credible coach. The International Coach Federation (ICF) is a leading organization that provides independent certification and sets the professional standards by which life coaches should practice. Currently, life coaching is not a regulated profession.

COMMON MISCONCEPTIONS OF LIFE COACHES

Life coaches are talented and help make the lives of many people better through their efforts. In this section, we will clarify some of the misconceptions that exist so you can fully understand what you are getting into. Life coaching encompasses many different things, but there are also many things it is not.

Life Coaching Is Not Counseling or Therapy

Many individuals conflate life coaching by comparing the practice to psychology, psychiatry, or other form of therapy. While it can intertwine with these areas, it is not the same thing. A therapist is a licensed professional that helps individuals with current or past issues of the mind and helps them overcome trauma. Life coaches deal with a person's present circumstances and assist them in building a future.

Life coaches definitely do not treat mental health disorders or give any type of medical advice. If this becomes apparent during a session, the coach should immediately refer the client to a therapist if they are not already seeing one. Most life coaching clients are healthy and successful, but they feel stuck or want more from their lives. They want to grow personally and professionally.

While there was once a lot of tension between life coaches and therapists, mainly because therapists felt coaches were stepping on their toes by practicing without a license, the attitude has started to change. One of the reasons is the whole "practicing therapy without a license" is false. Second, therapists have adopted an "if you can't beat them, join them" attitude. Many have recognized the need for coaching and have transitioned into this practice themselves. If you are working with a practitioner of both, the relationship needs to be made clear in regard to what you need. The therapist/life coach also needs to be straightforward about what service they are providing so the client does not become confused.

Life Coaching Is a Real Profession

Many people see life coaching as a hobby or side hustle. However, it is a real career and passion. They are able to help many people improve their lives and can create a lot of business doing so. If you decide to become a life coach, think of yourself as your own business person.

Life Coaches Do Not Need Training

Life coaches do not need to be certified; however, if you want to have long-term success in the field, going through a good training program is essential. You must learn the appropriate methods and communication strategies that will be beneficial to your clients. Otherwise, you could lead them astray, overstep your boundaries, or just not be helpful in any way. Life coaching is not just about speaking and telling people what to do. You must also know what to say, when to say it, and how to make it effective. You must also be a great listener so you can determine your client's needs.

The general public also trusts coaches who have certification. They feel their help will be more appropriate and beneficial. In a survey done by the International Coaching Federation (ICF), 84% of coaching clients stated in the affirmative when asked whether or not they care if their life coaches are certified (Stewart, 2014). If you want a successful life coaching practice, getting certified will be a positive investment.

Not All Coaches Are Slimy

Because the profession is not currently regulated, anyone can put up a sign and call themselves a life coach. They don't go through any training, don't learn any of the skills, and are only in it for a cash grab. That being said, there are many fine, reputable, and highly trained coaches out there. You just have to do your research. Remember, there are unethical people in every profession. You cannot judge the whole field by a few bad apples.

Coaching Is for Everyone

Coaching first started catching on when movie stars, high-level executives, and billionaires began using them. Over the years, the effectiveness of life coaching has become apparent. Coaches now specialize in helping people through all walks of life, so no matter what position you are in, there is a life coach available to help you.

WHY YOU SHOULD BECOME A LIFE COACH

Coaching

Life coaching is a dynamic profession that continues to grow and prosper. With so many individuals realizing the benefits it can have for them, there are no real signs of slowing down. The reason for writing this book is not just to tell you about how life coaching can help you, but encourage you to become one yourself if you choose. If you have liked the information thus far, consider taking this on as a passion. It can benefit you, and others, in many significant ways. We will go more in depth into the different types of coaching and specific techniques a person can utilize. Before getting there, let's go over some reasons why life coaching might be a perfect fit for you.

. . .

You Love Helping People

Are you someone who is always helping people? Do people feel safe coming to you with their problems? Are you the go-to person to help resolve an issue? Are you a great listener who truly hears someone out before responding? If so, life coaching might be right up your alley. Life coaches contribute a lot to help people live better lives, and you will have the opportunity to do this if you follow down this path. As you help others, you will help yourself too. Life coaches learn a lot from their clients, as well.

You Need a Higher Purpose by Helping Others

Do you find yourself in a field that is not satisfying to you? Are you just going through the motions to get a paycheck? Do you have a desire to serve other people? Life coaching gives you a great opportunity to serve others, which will also give you a higher purpose in life. Not only that, once your clientele grows, you can replace the income of a job that gives you no meaning.

You Help People Line up With Their Values

One of the things coaches help their clients with is to recall and understand their true values and beliefs in life. From there, they can help the client set up their goals according to these values. Imagine being able to help someone figure out their life's work. This can become a reality for you as a life coach.

. . .

You Value Time and Freedom

The great thing about life coaching is that you can do it from anywhere and at any time. You can have clients from all over the world and help them out over the phone or during a video conference call. You can assist one of your clients in the morning at your local coffee shop, then have a Skype call with someone in the afternoon that lives in another country. You can even talk to clients while you're vacationing on a cruise or staying at a resort by the beach. With life coaching, you will have the time and freedom to work when you want and where you want. Trade in that nine-to-five structured lifestyle and become an independent coach while helping so many people. You will be your own boss and won't have to answer to anyone.

Don't Do It for the Money

I am going to be upfront with you. Life coaching has the potential to bring in a lot of money. Some of the top coaches out there charge hundreds of dollars per hour. I am not guaranteeing these wages, but it's certainly possible. I don't want your focus to be on the money, though. Pay attention to your clients' needs, build relationships, and help as many people as you can, and eventually the finances will start flowing in.

Now that we have provided a general overview of what life coaching is, we will get into some more specific topics.

COMMON CHALLENGES OF LIFE COACHING

I admit we are a little biased here at Elvin Coaches because we love the life coaching profession. We have seen with our own eyes the many people who have changed their lives after getting the help of a great coach. The practice is valuable and we understand that. We all hope that you do too. That being said, this section will be dedicated to some of the challenges related to life coaching. These are not meant to be a deterrent. Our hope is that you will go into life coaching as a profession and a passion. We just want you to be fully informed before making the dive. This is something we would do during a coaching session and will make sure we do it here, as well.

- Building a trusting relationship. Before dismissing your client as uncoachable, determine if you've done enough to build a relationship where they trust you. Trust is essential for a good coach and client interaction.
- Avoid doing the heavy lifting. Your job as a coach is to ask the right questions and help your clients seek out answers. If they aren't coming up with solutions on their own, do not jump in, no matter how tempting it is. That is not your job as a coach. Keep asking follow-up questions until you get somewhere.
- Making your client reliant on you. Once again, this happens when you solve their problems for them.

They need to do it on their own. You do not want your client to become reliant on you. You actually want them to need you as little as possible, as crazy as that may sound.

- Having a client who thinks they know everything is a major issue. It can make the coach feel like they're obsolete. Arrogant people like this are not coachable. Arrogant people need to be challenged with some tough questions that make them open up more. If they continue to dismiss your help, you can only go so far. Save your energy for someone who will appreciate you.
- Clients can sometimes refuse to take action. Successful coaching is about giving accountability to the person being coached. If they are unwilling to set goals and take the proper steps, you can explore new goals with them, push them to make a commitment, or eventually break ties if none of the above work.

Life coaching definitely has its challenges, and some clients will be harder to break through than others. However, when you are dealing with a challenging situation with a client who is at the lowest point in their lives, watching them turn around and pick themselves back up is one of the greatest highs you will receive.

KEEPING IT PRIVATE

Security

A major theme throughout this book will be the idea of trust. Trust is extremely important in a coach-client relationship, and without it, no progress will be made. As a life coach, your client will reveal things about themselves that their best friends and closest family members may not know. They trust you with this information, and you need to take this very seriously.

Even though you are not expected to deal with medical issues, you must handle what your clients tell you in the same manner as protected health information. Therefore, everything they tell you must stay between the coach and the client. Respecting privacy is essential. If you don't, all trust will be lost, and rightfully so.

2

THE INTUITIVE COACH

"Intuition is always right in at least two ways; It is always in response to something. It always has your best interest at heart."

— GAVIN DE BECKER

We all have intuition, which can also be called a gut feeling. It is the ability to understand or feel something immediately, without the need for conscious reasoning, like when you are about to walk down a certain street but get an uncomfortable vibe about it. It is important to listen to our intuition because it is trying to tell us something our conscious mind may not be aware of.

An intuitive life coach is someone who can guide you on the right path and reach your goals by helping you access your intuition. This part of your psyche knows a lot about you, and you will learn a lot about yourself by paying attention to it. The ultimate objective of an intuitive coach is the same as any regular coach; they just have some different strategies. In addition to the secular elements of life, like habits, mind blocks, goal-setting, and action steps, they also bring in some spiritual principles into their practice so you can tap into your divine energy. This is to help you connect with the deepest parts of yourself, which you may have never even been aware of.

During your sessions with an intuitive coach, you can expect to be challenged to confront the issues that have been holding you back your whole life. Clients who are not used to this can become very uncomfortable during these moments. Confronting your limiting beliefs is never easy, but absolutely necessary if you want to heal. Once you are able to do this, you will fully recognize your strengths, weaknesses, and various issues you need to overcome. This can provide much guidance as you follow the path to living the life of your dreams.

An intuitive coach will generally work with the energy you give off. This will help them guide you in resolving your deepest issues. The energy you are projecting is coming from your intuition, which will let the coach know what your blockages are. After this, they can assist you in developing new thoughts, habits, and beliefs that support the life you really want and not the one you are pretending to love. Once you are past these issues, you can open yourself up to all of the opportunities that exist for you. Life has so much to offer all of us, and the intuitive life coach can help us realize that.

BENEFITS OF WORKING WITH AN INTUITIVE LIFE COACH

After working with an intuitive life coach, you will be able to adjust your thoughts and feelings so that they vibrate at a frequency that matches your desired life. We are all filled with thoughts that can sabotage our lives, and we don't even realize it. However, thoughts lead to actions, and actions lead to results. So, if our thoughts are limiting, our results will be too. If our thoughts are destructive, our results will be too. The proper life coach can help you nip them in the bud.

Through intuitive life coaching, you will get to know yourself better on a spiritual level. This does not mean you will start following a certain religion or deity. Of course, that could end up being the case. However, spirituality goes well beyond religion and has a much deeper meaning for most people. There are so many things you can get out of intuitive life coaching, like finding your purpose in life, discovering your dream career, healing past relationships, and learning what you really want in life. Perhaps you have been stuck in your hometown and determine you need to leave. This might be the place where all of your painful memories exist, and an intuitive life coach can help you figure it out. The following are a few other things that can happen for you while working under an intuitive life coach:

- Develop a new passion in life that you never even knew you were interested in.
- Take up some new hobbies that give meaning to your life. Some of these can even turn into a new career path.
- Achieve financial abundance by tapping into an unknown skill.
- Start a new business based on your passion.
- Become healthier and happier as a person.
- Discover how to listen more to your intuition.
- Live a better life overall.

You will receive a tremendous amount of benefits from intuitive life coaching, many of which you won't even realize until you go through it. You will be amazed at how much you learn about yourself. If you are unsure if you need help this type of life coach, do a self-assessment and determine if you have any of these feelings on a regular basis:

- Anger
- Resentment
- Unfulfillment
- Shame
- Depression

- Emptiness
- Jealousy
- Loneliness
- Lack of motivation
- Confusion

While everyone has these emotions at some point in their lives, they should never dominate your psyche. If they do, major changes need to be made. It might be time to work with an intuitive life coach, who can work on improving your self-love, confidence, and worldview.

METHODS OF AN INTUITIVE LIFE COACH

While intuitive life coaches are not medical practitioners, they do possess their own methods of healing that are beneficial to anybody. There can be many reasons why a person would need healing, including past trauma, dysfunctional relationships, bad career choices, or poor self-care. The focus of their practices is holistic techniques to help rebuild the body and mind. The methods can include:

- Hypnotherapy: This is when hypnosis is done for therapeutic purposes and helps clients initiate change on the subconscious level.
- Crystal healing: The use of crystals and gemstones to

absorb negative energy and replace it with positive energy.
- Reiki: A touch healing method that originates from Japan. The practitioner manipulates and channels energy into the client's body to create a balance within the body and mind.
- Chakra healing: This originates from India and is based on the idea that humans have a number of energy fields, known as chakras, which relate to different portions of the body. The knowledge of these energetic centers is used to establish balance and harmony.

While all of these practices are a part of intuitive life coaching, it is not a necessity for the field. A person's intuition can be accessed without these specific healing techniques. However, if you plan on becoming an intuitive life coach, consider learning these methods for effective energy manipulation. If you end up going down this path, you will be able to help people with their relationships, career, health, passion, self-love, confidence, creativity, spirituality, and pretty much every aspect of their lives.

Still Not Therapy

When we talk about intuitive life coaches being healers, people will assume that they're therapists. However, as we mentioned earlier, life coaches are not therapists in any way because they cannot diagnose illnesses or deal with any pathologies of the mind. The healing practices are centered around improving energy and are not related to clinical healing. If an intuitive life coach ever feels like they're dealing with significant mental disorders, they should be referring their clients to a licensed practitioner of therapy.

In addition to not treating specific disorders, an intuitive life coach will never tell you what to do with your life. That is not for them to decide, but they will help guide you in making your own decisions. An intuitive coach will also motivate you, but never force you to make changes or aggressively push you into taking action steps. Once again, that is up to you. Finally, they will not predict your circumstances. The future is uncertain and none of us know what will truly happen. However, we can set ourselves up as much as we can to build our lives as we desire.

LAW OF ATTRACTION

The basis of the Law of Attraction is that what we put out into the universe is what we ultimately attract. Our thoughts put out our specific energy, and that energy comes back to us in a similar fashion. For example, if we are thinking about excess wealth, good health, and positive relationships, the universe will hear this and we will have an abundance of these in our lives. Even if we are thinking about something in the negative, like if we are thinking about not living in poverty, we will still attract it because it is in our minds and therefore that's the energy we are putting out.

Negative emotions send off negative vibrations. Emotions like sadness, anger, shame, or hatred will snowball, and you will create more of these within yourself. On the other hand, positive emotions will do the same thing. Therefore, if you are happy, peaceful, and motivated, the vibrations you give off will attract more of these emotions.

Many intuitive life coaches subscribe to the idea of the Law of Attraction. They can help their clients change their thoughts from negative to positive, so they only attract more of these later on. In this manner, they are using the Law of Attraction to their advantage.

While people don't deserve bad things to happen to them because they are thinking negatively, it certainly is an explanation of why unhealthy emotions beget further unhealthy emotions.

The Law of Attraction can be targeted toward any area of your life, whether money, career, relationships, or success. The Universe is much smarter than we give it credit for, and if you want it to be on your side, give it some good vibes. This particular law does not discriminate based on age, race, gender, or cultural background. Simply put, what you focus on is what you will get. It may not happen right away, but ultimately, as the mind thinketh, the universe giveth.

In some form or another, the Law of Attraction has existed for centuries. Most of the major religions, like Christianity, Judaism, or Buddhism, have incorporated the philosophy into their teachings. Hence, this is not a new phenomenon. While the exact mechanism is not fully understood, many scientists such as quantum physicists have given more insight into the scientific basis of the law. As individuals, we do not have to understand the details; we just have to recognize how the law works. Once we do, our life will be filled with abundance.

To clear things up a little bit, the Law of Attraction is not some type of magic wand. It does not mean that if you imagine a pile of money, hundred-dollar bills will start falling from the sky. However, if your focus is on financial wealth, the universe will present more opportunities to make money.

Now that you understand the law, start making it work for you. Transition your thoughts so you stop thinking about all of the negative things in life. Instead, paint a picture in your mind about your ideal circumstances. Be specific about where you want to live, the friends you want around you, and the career you want to have. Use real-life visuals, like pictures, positive quotes written down, or screensavers on your computer to keep these positive images in your mind.

Once your thoughts automatically veer towards the positive, you will eventually have an abundance of things you want. It really is that simple, but it won't be easy. It takes constant effort to steer your mind away from negative thinking, but once you are living your dream life, it will all be worth it. Once again, work with an intuitive life coach that can help you with the Law of Attraction.

If you are someone who enjoys working with energy and believes in the power of intuition, consider going down this career path. Just like with general coaching, you will be able to make a difference in so many people's lives and use your own unique talents for healing purposes. You will also have the time and freedom to work from anywhere at any time you want.

In the next chapter, we will get into more coaching techniques that are powerful, effective, and elicit change.

3

POWERFUL COACHING TECHNIQUES AND SKILLS

Ideas!

While any average Joe can stake out a location and call themselves a life coach, they will ultimately get exposed for the frauds that they are. We just hope too many people do not get harmed in the process. The bottom line is, life coaching takes a certain amount of skill and talent in order to perform effectively. A person must also have the right mindset, which is to help people. This can also be developed over time, but is beneficial to have as the reason for going into this field.

The focus of this chapter will be the proper techniques and skills needed to be a great life coach. There are reasons why Tony Robbins, John Maxwell, Wayne Dyer, and Brian Tracy get a lot of clients. They utilize techniques that are effective and well-respected. Many people, including those at the top of their field, seek out these professionals to help them in the darkest moments of their lives. We mentioned several of the celebrities in the previous chapter who relied on the help of life coaches during their dark periods.

Life coaching is a serious practice that is gaining more steam every day. When you become a life coach, I want you to realize that people will put a lot of their faith and trust into you. I hope that you take this trust very seriously. I hope you take the life coaching profession, as a whole, very seriously and receive the proper training that you will need.

THE TECHNIQUES YOU NEED FOR GREAT COACHING

> "The only difference between the master and the novice is that the master has failed more times than the novice has tried."
>
> — STEPHEN MCCRANIE

Mastering anything in life does not happen overnight. It takes years of continuous practice to become a master, and once you get to that level, there is still more to learn. The point here is, life coaching will take time to master. In fact, you may practice this art for many years and still not master it. You may become good, even great, but that still won't make you a master. The objective is to never stop learning and growing. Also, never believe you know it all because trust me, none of us do.

As a life coach, you will have to make time to hone your skills, have the patience to never give up, and practice incessantly. Finally, you will need to work on mastering specific coaching techniques. Once you do, they will become your best friend and greatest resource. You cannot function as a life coach without some baseline methods. Even though you will become more creative and individualize techniques based on the client's needs, you still need a foundation to keep you grounded. In the end, this will be the ultimate deciding factor for your success. All of the other factors are just icing on the cake.

TECHNIQUES THAT WILL BENEFIT YOUR CLIENTS

There are numerous coaching techniques that a life coach will have at their disposal. If you get training at various academies for this field, you will probably learn different techniques. Many of these will have varying names, but the same course of action. I will go over some effective coaching techniques in this section that you can benefit from yourself, then use on clients when you get to that point.

The Wheel of Life Coaching Technique

The objective of this practice is to help a client take an honest, non-judgmental look at their current circumstances in life and focus on their most important areas. No matter how much discipline a person has, life continues to change and evolve, which causes them to stop paying attention to the important areas of their life. Priorities grow, change, and evolve constantly, and this can cause life to get away from a person. After a while, issues that are not vital to our lives and that we don't want anything to do with take up most of our time. The Wheel of Life coaching technique will help your client gain or regain a sense of direction, purpose, and balance. They will, once again, realize what really matters to them in life.

To begin using this technique, use the following steps:

- Ask your client to draw a regular circle on a piece of paper.
- Divide the circle into eight sections, like a pizza or a pie. Then label each section the following:
- Family and friends
- Romance
- Personal growth
- Business/career
- Finances
- Health
- Fun and recreation
- Physical environment
- Now, ask the client to label each section on a scale of one to 10, based on their satisfaction level. If they put zero, they are not satisfied at all. Write these numbers down on each separate segment.
- Once they have these items ranked, ask the client to start with the weakest areas of their lives, according to their own assessment, and come up with about three ways to boost each category. For example, if romance is a weak point, perhaps they can set aside 30 minutes every night and dedicate it to their spouse or partner if they have one.

The wheel of life provides a visual of a client's current reality and dream reality. Not only that, but it also forces them to come up with action steps to reach their desired life. If a client feels a lack of balance in their lives, this tool will help identify where the imbalance is. For instance, your career might be going perfectly, but your health and relationships might be suffering.

Popular motivational speaker and author Larry Winget heavily criticizes people who do not have a written plan for every area of their lives. This is why their work, health, relationships, and mind suffer continuously. When Mr. Winget is asked why people are poor, unhealthy, and miserable, his answer usually goes along the lines of, "Because they choose to be." You have to choose a better life by focusing on all areas. As he said, have a written down plan for all of these areas. The wheel chart can be your plan.

This tool does not have to be limited to eight sections. You can break it down even further. Also, you can create a wheel chart for specific areas of your life. For example, you can focus on your career or business and break it down into different areas that need to be addressed. This type of strategy should be done whenever you feel your life is not going in the proper direction.

The Moonshot Coaching Technique

Moonshot

Many individuals feel trapped in a routine that is meaningless, but they keep doing it on a daily basis because they feel like they can't do anything else. Also, it is easy to live this way because they don't have to evolve or challenge themselves in any way. They can simply live mindlessly and perform the same mundane practices day after day and year after year.

We've got some news for you. This is not really living, and if you decide to create your life this way, you will never grow, prosper, or create the life you have always wanted. You might as well be living as a zombie at this point.

"Don't live the same year 75 times and call it a life."

— ROBIN SHARMA

The Moonshot coaching technique is perfect for those clients who have lost their sense of adventure and excitement for life. People in this category would never live their lives off the cuff, even for a day. They would rather wake up and live the same boring existence from the day before with as little unpredictability as possible. As a life coach, your job is to help these individuals get out of the funk they are in. Help them realize once again how exciting life can be and how one day does not have to match the rest.

To perform this effective technique, take the following steps:

- Ask your client a series of challenging and unorthodox questions to get them out of their current mindset. Some examples include:
- What is a common dream that you always have?
- Are you ever jealous of what those around you are doing?
- What things excite you about life?
- If money was not an issue, what would be doing right now?
- Once they have answered these questions, have them

create a list of things they would love to be, have, and do. Don't limit them on what they can write down. Allow their imaginations to run free. Do they want to go to Mars? If so, they need to write it down. These are known as Moonshot Goals.
- After making their list, ask them to pick their top three which are big, but completely attainable.
- Work with your client to break down each goal into smaller and achievable steps. This will make the goal seem less daunting.

After practicing these strategies, the client should have a new thought process about how to live life. They will start changing their routines and be okay with challenging themselves. When a person gets out of their comfort zone, real growth starts to occur.

The Spheres of Influence Coaching Technique

There are many people who can't get a hold of their lives simply because they are overwhelmed with so many things. They become helpless and unsure of where to go or what to do. As a result, they spend an exorbitant amount of time and energy trying to work through problems, situations, and challenges they have no control over. They might not realize their lack of control because there is too much going on to remain focused. With the Sphere of Influence coaching technique, your client will realize that there are things they cannot control, so they should not waste energy doing so, and they should rather focus their attention on things they can control and influence.

Once individuals follow this technique, they will gain a lot of insight into what to walk away from. They will realize that the world's problems are not theirs to take on. To start implementing this technique, use the following steps:

- Have your client draw a large circle and then a smaller circle inside of it.
- In the smallest circle, have them write, "Things I can control." In the space between the large and small circle, have them write, "Things I can influence." Finally, outside of the large circle, have them write, "Everything else."
- Now, walk them through the individual challenges that they are struggling with. What is causing them to feel overwhelmed?
- As they are listing their problems, help them determine which part of the drawing each specific one needs to go into. For example, if a person is worried about losing their job, they can list the reason for their anxiety and worry in the following fashion.
- Things they can't control: The state of the economy, such as if the company is downsizing.
- Things they can influence: Developing better communication with their boss to determine what they

need to do to keep their job. This does not mean kissing up or stooging on other employees.
- Things they can control: Building up their resume, searching for new jobs just in case, and reaching out to their network for possible opportunities.

This coaching technique will give your clients a clear view of any situation. They will realize what they can and can't control or influence, and therefore will become less overwhelmed and more focused. They will have a sense of perspective to come up with new ideas for growth and opportunities.

4

THE TIME TRAVEL COACHING TECHNIQUE

(GRUSHNIKOV, N.D.)

We are not talking about real time travel here. At least, not yet. However, we are talking about looking into the future. Many people have not taken steps to build the life they want because they are anxious about what will happen if they do. As a result, people are stuck in dead-end jobs because they can't bear the possibility of not having an income, remain in toxic relationships because they are worried about not having friends, or don't travel to a place they've always wanted to go because they are terrified of what might happen to them.

With the Time Travel coaching technique, you will guide your client in traveling to the future in an imaginary world and envision what their life could be like if they followed their dreams. To use this technique:

- Have your clients picture themselves in the future, anywhere from a few months to 10 years down the line. Then ask them some specific questions:
- What does your life look like? What do you see and hear? What does your daily routine look like from start to finish? Where do they live?
- Ask them if their imaginary picture is vastly different from what they have.
- Help them come up with smaller goals to attain the big picture goal they have in their mind.

This technique will help a client build some clarity around their values, desires, and goals.

The Eisenhower Matrix Coaching Technique

Some major obstacles to success are prioritizations, time management, and productivity. All of these factors tie in to each other. They ultimately result in how well and efficiently you are able to complete something. No matter what you decide to do in life, whether it's entrepreneurship, working for a company, or being a stay-at-home parent, you will need to be able to handle things in a timely manner. Even your health and relationships can be affected by poor time management, productivity, and prioritization. For example, if your family is not getting an adequate amount of your attention, they might grow to resent you.

Before you can use the Eisenhower Matrix coaching technique, you must explain to your clients the difference between urgent and important.

- Urgent: This is anything that requires immediate attention. These situations generally don't have time to wait and put people into a reactive and defensive state. Urgent issues are generally tasks related to other people's goals.
- Important: This is anything that contributes to long-term gains. These types of issues put people in a responsive state where they have a sense of control and clarity.

Urgency!

After defining these terms, get out a piece of paper and draw a matrix, which should be one large square with four smaller quadrants inside of it. On the outer edges of the square, write 'urgent' above the first quadrant and 'important' to the left of it. Write "not urgent" above the second quadrant. For the third quadrant, write "not important" on the outside of it to the left. After this, label the inside of each quadrant the following:

- Quadrant 1: Do
- Quadrant 2: Plan
- Quadrant 3: Delegate
- Quadrant 4: Eliminate

Once the full matrix has been drawn, you will now have the client fill in the necessary information.

- Quadrant 1: Urgent and important issues. These can include things like getting an important project done

for work, a major repair done on your home, or picking up the medications that you ran out of from the pharmacy.
- Quadrant 2: These are not urgent, but important tasks. These can be activities like going to the bank, buying groceries for the week, or calling a friend back who left you a message.
- Quadrant 3: These are urgent and not important. This might sound like an oxymoron, but hear us out. These are tasks that need to be quick but don't really carry a lot of weight, for example attending work meetings or replying to emails.
- Quadrant 4: These are not urgent or important tasks, for example scrolling through social media, playing video games, and watching TV.

After establishing what each quadrant is in detail, it is now time to prioritize them.

- Quadrant 1 tasks need to be done now with no delays.
- Quadrant 2 tasks can be planned for later on.
- Quadrant 3 tasks can probably be delegated.
- Quadrant 4 tasks can be deleted completely. Only do these after the first three quadrants are taken care of.

When you create and follow this grid, you will know what activities in your life require the most amount of attention.

From here, you will have much more clarity about what your goals should be.

All of these coaching techniques are effective in their own way and are the solutions for different problems a person might have. You may end up using one or a combination of all of these methods to help your client out. It's great to practice and be aware of all of these strategies because you never know when you might use them.

TECHNIQUES TO CREATE MORE IMPACT

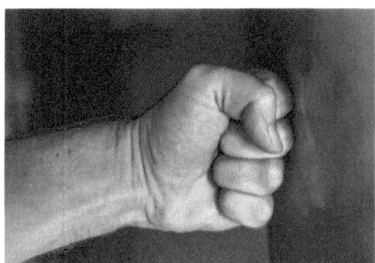

We will go over some more impactful coaching techniques that will really start a mindset shift for your clients. You will really start seeing a transformation within your clients and how they view the world. There are four specific techniques with a simple strategy, but powerful results.

Technique 1

The first technique is called "The Perfect Day Exercise." Many clients live the same day over and over again and don't realize they can have something better. They can live a more purposeful life. As many of us get older, we forget how to daydream like we once did. As children, you might have been told to stop daydreaming and get back to reality. We are giving you permission to start doing this again, and tell your clients to do the same thing.

During the daydreaming phase, we are often imaging what our ideal life will be like. Of course, when we are five or six, we picture ourselves as superheroes, dinosaurs, or other mythical figures. As we get older, we start imagining what our perfect life will consist of. In many cases, the influential adults in our lives tell us to take a structured path filled with certainty and security. While these adults had our best interest at heart, they also severely limited our potential. As the years went by, we forgot our true dreams and desires, and instead focused on making a living.

The perfect day exercise gets us back into daydreaming and picturing what our ideal or perfect day looks like. When you have your clients practice this technique, have them write down in detail what they want to do throughout the day. What kind of career will they have? How early do they want to get up each day? At what time will their workday end? How many hours a day will they spend with family? What types of hobbies will they have? Where is their ideal place to live? These and many more questions should be answered by your client. You want them to be as detailed as possible.

Writing it down can help them visualize and remember their perfect day.

The goal of this exercise is not just to figure out what they want their lives to be like, but to help them realize the mindset shift that needs to occur. Finally, ask your client what is holding them back. You might be surprised by their responses, and they will be too. This final question can significantly change how your client approaches their work and daily routines. Instead of just existing, they may start living with the intent of changing.

You will be amazed at the perfect life your clients come up with and how they can be vastly different from their reality. For example, an unassuming accountant with a nine-to-five schedule might have a passion for music and the dream of being a guitar player. The perfect day exercise can give you a lot of surprises and can be a fun technique to employ.

Technique 2

The second technique involves using a coaching journal. It is estimated that the human mind has about 60,000 to 80,000 thoughts in a single day (Mindvalley, n.d.). Broken down, that's about 40-55 thoughts in a minute, so our minds are being inundated every moment of the day. It's impossible to recall all of these thoughts. In fact, most people forget them immediately and never pay attention to them again. The issue is, many of these thoughts could have given us deep insights about ourselves and the world we live in. The mind may have been trying to tell us something on the subconscious level, as well.

Having a coaching journal allows a person to keep their thoughts straight and recollect them later on. It is hard to process everything in our psyche in real time. Therefore, if you journal your thoughts throughout the day, you can revisit them any time and see where your mind wandered to.

As a coach, having your client utilize this technique can help all parties understand their true feelings. Our emotions in real time give us deep insight into what we want out of life. They can even give us a clue as to what we find repulsive. For example, if your client started feeling angry or depressed out of nowhere, he or she may not recognize it when it happened, but can look back on their journal and find out that these feelings occurred while they were around a certain group of people. On the other hand, if the person was extremely happy at a certain point, they can determine what was making them feel that way at that moment.

Ask your client to share their journal with you during the sessions. You can help them decipher what is going on and see if there is a pattern of thoughts that need to be addressed. Journaling is a powerful technique. Your clients can carry around a small notepad or even use a program on their phones. We realize it is not realistic to be journaling at every moment of the day, but have them do it whenever they get some downtime to recollect their emotions.

Technique 3

Check-in

At the beginning of each coaching session, you need to have a check-in with your client, and at the end of the session, you must have a check-out. These strategies can determine how well your interactions will go on any particular day. Many coaches ignore these practices, but they are essential for a positive session. The check-ins allow your client to drop any baggage from the outside world so they can be fully present during the coaching session. They can mention and then let go of any anger, anxiety, frustration, depression, and other negative emotions they might be carrying around. The coach is able to gauge where the client is coming from at this point, and they will both have a greater understanding during their interaction.

For the check-out, the coach and client will determine what action steps need to be taken to create some actual changes. While a client can leave a session feeling very motivated, it can go away really quickly once life starts to happen. Suddenly, everything that was gone over during the coaching session is gone forever and it will be back to square one again. A good check-out moment will allow the coach to see how effective the session was and how likely the client is to take real action. Having concrete steps to be held accountable for can make a client more likely to use the information they gained from a life coach. As a coach, you can also have certain goals and milestones that need to be completed by the next session.

Never skip the check-in and check-out. Take these moments to pause and make sure you are on the same page as your client.

Check-out

Technique 4

The final technique here is called the "what scares me?" technique. This process is pretty simple. Have your client write down all of their fears. Have them dig deep down and not just focus on superficial fears, like being afraid of the dark or spiders. Ask them what scares them at their core, like having a fear of failure, being alone, or letting their family down. What truly terrifies them in life to the point it becomes crippling?

Once you determine their fears, you can assess how much of their life is driven by them. Many of these exist on the subconscious level and are rooted in something mysterious, like a past trauma. Once the client's list is done, tackle each fear one at a time.

These techniques are effective for your coaching sessions, and you will make real progress with your clients. Once you begin mastering these skills, your clients will benefit a lot from you, and you will become a highly sought out coach in your field.

TECHNIQUES REQUIRING MORE SKILL

There are certain advanced techniques that some coaches will use, either because they were involved in a different field before coaching and had these skills beforehand, or they learned them to complement their coaching strategy. Whatever the case, you are not required to have these skills, but can choose to learn them if you want. I will go over these techniques to give you an idea of what they're about. From here, you can choose to incorporate them into your sessions or not. I will say that training in these methods can help you become more empowered as a life coach and help resolve more problem areas for your client.

Neuro-Linguistic Programming

This is a psychological approach used by individuals that involves analyzing, and eventually applying, strategies of successful people. As a life coach, you can use neuro-linguistic programming to help clients change their language and behavior techniques. Once they start mimicking the habits of successful people, they will start realizing their full potential.

Emotional Freedom Technique

Emotional freedom technique (EFT) is a form of acupuncture that does not use needles. Instead, the fingertips are used to access and stimulate the various energy points on the body. EFT is a great New Age method for dispelling excess emotional pain.

As a coach, you can also train in hypnotherapy to reach your patient while they are in a more relaxed state of being. From here, you can help your client become more motivated in breaking poor behavioral and cognitive patterns.

You will find that some of your clients have a very hard time expressing their feelings verbally. In these cases, you can have them perform writing exercises. Many people find it easier to be more clear and honest while writing than they are with speaking.

Cognitive Behavioral Coaching

This is not the same as cognitive behavioral therapy, which requires more of a psychological approach, similar to psychotherapy. Cognitive behavioral coaching is more about looking at a client's present thoughts and trying to improve them for the future. Basically, a coach will assist in replacing negative thought patterns with positive ones. As a coach, you will not be dealing with dysfunctions or mental health disorders. If this is necessary, you may have to refer your client to a licensed therapist.

Guided Meditation

Meditation is a truly powerful exercise that can help people become more mindful and less stressed, as well as reducing mental blocks. There are many books, classes, and practitioners that teach proper meditation techniques. You can even watch videos on YouTube to learn some simple methods. It can take years for people to master meditation practices, so learning the basics is good enough for your sessions. As a coach, you can guide your clients through meditation until they can do it on their own.

OTHER EFFECTIVE TECHNIQUES

I will end this chapter by going over some other effective techniques a coach can use during their sessions. These are also simple but work well.

Evidence Hunting

This is when you hunt for evidence throughout your life that shows the possibility of success in the future. A coach can help their client look for this evidence.

Perspective Change

The way a person experiences life has a lot to do with how they perceive things. Sometimes, the items we overly focus on can make our lives seem much grimmer than they actually are. Changing our perspective will bring new thoughts, which can give us a completely different outcome. As humans, we have a tendency to look at the negative side of everything, but a life coach can help us to refocus on the better parts of less favorable experiences and help us learn from them. This does not mean you are ignoring reality, just choosing to pay attention to the positive aspects of it.

Positive Affirmations

Positive affirmations are a way to reinforce your beliefs with more confidence and thus remove many negative internalized beliefs. We often have preconceived limitations on what we can handle. Affirmations like these can help back us up in times of belief crisis. A good life coach can help their clients come up with affirmations related to their goals and values.

All of these coaching techniques are powerful in their own way. Your clients will benefit from them greatly as they help solve their own unique problems. That best part is, they truly help coached clients find hidden answers within themselves.

5

TYPES OF COACHING STYLES

There is more than one way to skin a cat. There is always more than one route to get to a destination. If the door closes, go through a window. There are countless phrases and expressions out there to state the fact that there is no one way to do something. We all have our own styles that work best for us. This includes our coaching style. Despite following certain foundational rules, every life coach has their own personality. Some are more outspoken and aggressive, while others are soft-spoken and reserved.

As you come into your own as a coach, it is up to you what kind of style you utilize. Keep in mind that how your client takes you is important too. Different demeanors work better with various individuals and situations. You might have to change up your style every so often, and even within the same session, based on the progress you are making. The style you choose will have a remarkable impact on how your clients embrace your help. If they do not appreciate an aggressive approach, you must scale back and try something new. Being able to change up your methods is the only way to become a well-rounded life coach.

How you approach any coaching situation can literally make or break the rapport you have with a client. Your ultimate objective is to help them. Therefore, you must know how to gauge a situation well. The focus of this chapter will be the various coaching styles that exist and how they will work in various situations. Mastering the various coaching styles will make you an authority in the field and show your expertise to your clients. They will have more trust in you when they see that you have the ability to be flexible and change things up when needed. Confidence is attractive in a person, and whoever you work with as a coach will find you much more appealing in this regard.

Remember that a person is much more likely to take advice from someone who has their own life together. If you are scatter-brained, disorganized, and don't have anything in order, your clients will sense it immediately, and the relationship will become strained before eventually coming to an end.

THE COACHING APPROACH

Coaching styles are simply the social approaches and behavioral models that a life coach of any kind depends on for their personal brand and client needs. Some coaches develop a more authoritarian persona, while others create a friendly persona for themselves. Always understand that your reputation will precede you as a coach, so having multiple styles makes you a more effective and versatile coach.

Imagine that a pitcher in baseball throws the perfect curveball. He can strike out any right-handed player easily. However, this perfect curveball does not work well against someone who bats left-handed because the curve goes directly into their swing. Suddenly, the perfect pitch becomes useless, not because of the technique, but the situation itself. This holds true for your style as a coach, as well. No matter how excellent your methods are, if they don't mesh with a situation, they won't be effective.

If you are having a difficult time getting through to someone, don't automatically blame your coaching ability. It can be a matter of changing your approach.

Just like you don't need an actual certification for coaching, you do not need any licenses or certifications for the different coaching styles. Of course, the more training and experience you have, the better. The clients will also have more faith in you. Also, certain advanced techniques, like neuro-linguistic programming or hypnotherapy, require a certain level of knowledge to perform correctly. The general public is still skeptical about these certain techniques, and having some type of certification to back them up will give you more credibility. Look at it this way, how much trust would you have in someone who just walked up to you and said they know hypnotherapy?

We will now go over some coaching styles that you can incorporate into your coaching routine. Consider the advantages and disadvantages of each kind and how receptive different clients will be based on their personality. There is no one-size-fits-all approach, so it will behoove you to learn them all.

The Autocratic Style

Authoritarian

This is a highly structured coaching style where the control of the session lies squarely in the hands of the coach. The life coach acts like more of an authoritarian and develops a pre-established plan of action. With this method, the client is expected to follow the coach's lead without much room for deviation.

This type of style is used a lot for business coaching. The client will not receive a program tailor-made for them. The coach will be the authority figure, and the client must follow their directions.

This type of style works well for those who need discipline and structure. The client who needs immediate approaches to fix their circumstances will do well with an autocratic coach. As a coach, if you feel that your client needs to know exactly what is expected of them, use this practice to help them. If you give these individuals the freedom to come up with their own decisions, they will simply waver and fall into the abyss. Clients who respect authority will respect the autocratic coach.

To be an effective autocratic coach, you must encourage the following:

- Productivity
- Efficiency
- Trust in the coach
- Stress reduction
- Realistic goal attainment
- Reduced ambiguity

During urgent and pressing situations, the autocratic style reigns supreme above all else. This is because there is not much time for collaboration, and a single leader must take the helm. A person who wants to be told what to do, rather than guess, will appreciate listening to an authority figure.

The problem with this style is that a client can become overwhelmed and feel unheard. Even when a person wants you to take control, you still need to gauge the situation and allow them to make the final decision. Think of this as more of a structured approach to help the client come up with their own answers. That is what life coaching is all about.

Some people want to be in control of their lives and refuse to give up the reins to anyone else. This type of person will not benefit from an authoritarian style. If you are coaching someone with a strong personality who wants to make their own decisions, try a different method. There are plenty more to go over.

The Democratic Coaching Style

This type of style follows the same principles of a democracy. It takes into account the concerns, interests, and choices of the people involved. It is a much more inclusive and targeted approach than the strict autocratic style, and it allows room for more tailor-made programs. With this method, the client has a much bigger say in how the sessions go and in what way specific issues will be resolved. The client has as much control as the coach, or more.

The democratic style allows for a client to be introspective, have self-control, and be accountable for their decisions. Since they are the ones most in control, they assume much more accountability for the outcomes. Career coaching, financial coaching, and personal growth coaching are some examples where this style is most beneficial. These are the areas in life where a person needs more accountability.

This coaching style encourages the following:

- Motivation
- Teamwork and collaboration
- Self-efficacy
- Creativity
- Commitment to objectives
- Empowerment
- Productivity

If your client has a very hard time making decisions or has no clue what direction they should go, the democratic style might not be effective. The client will simply run around in circles without any real progress. The autocratic approach will be more appropriate in cases like these.

Holistic Coaching Style

You may have heard the term "holistic medicine," which views the whole person when providing medical treatment. It does not just focus on one area of the body or curing a single disease.

The holistic coaching style follows the same ideology in encompassing the whole person. The mindset of a holistic coach is that the body is one working unit and not a bunch of segmented parts. All areas must work in synchronicity with one another, or they will all cease to function at some point.

Therefore, a coach who follows this model must pay attention to their client's complete growth and encourage balance in all areas of their life. This is an ideal approach to use when you are getting to know a client because you will target all aspects of their being and really be able to figure out what their true strengths and weaknesses are.

The holistic style can provide a coaching client with perspective about their true place in the world. This will make them feel more connected, give them a sense of purpose, help them recognize why they matter, and understand how to get where they want to be.

Life coaches should strive to recognize their clients as a whole person. The holistic coaching style encourages the following benefits:

- Feeling understood
- Trust in the coach-client relationship
- Uncovering of feelings that are deeply held
- Enhanced well-being and functioning across the whole spectrum of a person and their life

This is a type of style that almost anyone will find appealing, especially when determining more in-depth issues that might be going on.

Laissez-Faire Coaching Style

This is the most hands-off coaching style, which works when a client has the ability to motivate themselves with minimal guidance from an outside source. In this approach, a life coach simply acts as a type of consultant who makes regular check-ups, but for the most part holds the client responsible as the primary owner of the process. Basically, the client comes up with their own methods of dealing with their issues, while the coach is available as a backup if needed.

The laissez-faire style has been criticized as being ineffective due to having zero leadership from the coach. Critics of this method point out the lack of leadership and responsibility as the coach shows virtually none of it during the process. However, proponents of this style feel it has a lot of value as long as there are regular performance follow-ups that are done. This style encourages the following:

- Self-empowerment
- Self-efficacy
- Self-management
- Freedom
- Decision-making abilities
- Autonomy

This style is probably not a good one to start off with and will work best with clients who have worked with a life coach for a while and are familiar with developing their own plans.

Transformational Coaching Style

This is a one-on-one approach that aims to build a trusting relationship between a coach and a client in which both parties agree upon the process and end goals. There is no hierarchy here as it is a 50-50 partnership. The coach will provide the authentic support and candid feedback when necessary.

This type of coaching style encourages the following:

- Collaborative skills
- Self-discovery
- Intrinsic motivation
- Accountability
- Problem-solving

Transactional Coaching

This is an exchanged-focused relationship between a coach and a client. It is aimed at promoting performance and getting rid of stumbling blocks. A few substyles of transactional coaching are rewards coaching, which is the offering of rewards for good performance; active management by exception, which is actively attending to the client's challenges; and passive management by exception, which is only intervening when problems become more advanced. Transactional coaching encourages:

- Problem-solving skills
- Performance enhancement
- Competency-building
- Goal clarity
- Short-term changes

Mindfulness Coaching

Mindfulness is the practice of becoming fully present in your situation. It means you are not thinking about the past or worrying about the future. You are simply at peace with the current moment. Mindfulness coaching draws from this philosophy by promoting a type of awareness in which a person starts paying attention to their present thoughts and feelings without any judgment.

The goal of this approach is to help a client respond to stress and anxiety in a calmer way. Mindfulness coaching encourages the following:

- Acceptance
- Peace of mind
- Clarity
- Reduced anxiety
- Awareness

- Harmony with the present moment.

There are more coaching styles that exist beyond the one mentioned here, but these are some of the most common ones practiced. Most clients you come across will benefit from one of these strategies, but as you move your coaching practice along, you may learn other methods for specific settings. Your personal coaching style will determine how you interact with your clients, so be aware of all of them and practice each one depending on what the situation calls for.

So far, we have gone over the life coaching process and various styles and techniques to make you the best in the field. Your clients will see you as an expert when you can change fluidly between various approaches and know when to use them accordingly. If you display uncertainty in your practices, your clients will be uncertain about you, which is not a good sign. There is still much more information to go over, so we are not done yet.

CHAPTER 5: GREAT QUESTIONS TO ASK WHEN COACHING SOMEONE

Questions?

As a life coach, you will be helping clients find many solutions in life. But instead of using the more orthodox manner of providing answers, you will instead be asking a lot more questions. These questions are meant to guide a conversation towards finding a solution, which the client will be able to come up with themselves. This will be a critical part of any coaching session, so you must know the right questions to ask, as well as how and when to ask them. The energy and demeanor you give off will set the tone for the interaction. Also, asking a brilliant question at the wrong time can be detrimental. You must gauge your client and determine what they are ready for.

The largest mistake life coaches make is trying to solve the problems for their clients. They are actually doing a disservice in this respect. People need to learn how to help themselves in order to get the best results in the long term. All of us have the answers to the challenges in our own life. We just need someone to point us in the right direction. Therefore, think of questions as directional points. If you guide someone into turning left when they should have gone right, they can end up on the wrong path. As you gain more experience, you will experience the power of asking the right questions.

You might have noticed that the first part of the word question is "quest," as in, you are on a 'quest' to find answers. This is why random questioning is not the way to go. There needs to be some sort of strategy involved.

MAKING A TRANSFORMATION

The magic of transformational coaching occurs when your client has foundational shifts in their neurology and thought process. Always remember that the work happens inside of your client's mind and not in your own mind. Use the following questions as a guide to help them uncover their personal solutions. We will break these down into separate sections.

Questions to Identify With Their Model of the World

Everyone has a different view of the world, and perception becomes reality. As a coach, it is important not to jump in with assumptions and automatically believe you understand someone and their issues. Also, never undercut what they are going through by making dismissive statements like, "You know, everyone has problems." While it's true, everyone has a unique set of circumstances that affect them differently.

Always create a positive rapport and a safe space for your clients. They should feel comfortable expressing their thoughts without the fear of judgment. With these questions, you are attempting to learn their model of the world, and not necessarily change it. For this to occur, you must come from a place of curiosity without actually jumping into their thoughts. The following are some great questions to help you identify with your client.

- What is the problem from your perspective?
- What is this particular problem making you say about yourself?
- What have you tried before in a similar situation that has worked, if anything?
- Similarly, what have you tried in a similar situation that has not worked?

- What are you telling yourself about the possible solutions?
- What are you really afraid of here? (Everyone has unique fears that may be vastly different than your own.)
- What beliefs do you have about yourself, in general?
- What beliefs do you have about the world, in general?
- What do you really want out of your life?
- What is really important to you?
- What habits do you currently possess that support your goals?
- What habits do you have that may sabotage your goals?

After asking these in-depth questions, you will have a great idea of how your client identifies with the world. You may learn things that surprise you and that you never even thought of. Remember, though, the questions are not about you, so just listen to the answers without any preconceived notions.

Questions for Getting Leverage and Permission

This relates to how ready the client is to make changes and how well you can convince them to do so. Before you enter this phase of questions, you must ensure your client is on board to move forward. If not, keep digging until you get to the necessary readiness for change. Once your client is at that point, proceed with these questions to get leverage:

- If you don't make this change, what will it mean to you?
- If you don't make this change, what will it cost you? (This is not about finances, but anything valuable in their lives.)
- What's missing in your life?
- Who in your life is missing out?
- Who else does your current pattern of behavior possibly hurt?
- When will you know that you have suffered enough?
- How will you know that you are ready to change now?

The remainder of the questions are geared for getting permission:

- Do you want to clear this up now? As in, are you ready to start taking action today, at this moment?
- Would you like help with this issue right now?
- Would you give me full permission to be your life coach and help you through this?
- Are you ready to access your unconscious mind to eliminate this problem and have conscious awareness of the change?

After these sets of questions, you will have full leverage and permission to help the person. Of course, that is if they agree to it.

Questions for Determining New Outcomes

Have your client clearly define their new desired outcomes. What do they want to be feeling, thinking, and experiencing, etc. when the coaching session is completed? Have them be crystal clear about their outcomes, and don't let them get away with being generalized. Make sure they are coming up with this on their own and you are not urging them in any direction. Even if you think a certain route will be better for them, only the client can decide this ultimately. The following are some great questions to ask for determining new outcomes:

- What are you not experiencing right now that you want to experience?
- What are you experiencing right now that you no longer want to experience?
- What would you like to happen for you?
- How do you want to feel?
- What would all of this look like?
- Paint me a picture of everything in your mind, and be as descriptive as possible. Who is there with you? What do you see all around you? What do you hear and smell? What can you touch? What are you thinking and not thinking? What emotions are you feeling on the inside?

OPEN-ENDED QUESTIONS

You may have noticed that most of these questions are open-ended rather than definitive, or closed. Closed-ended questions will result in abrupt answers with little to no opportunity for advancement. Open-ended questions allow you to seek out more answers with your client, which are more likely to lead to proper solutions. Avoid closed-ended questions like:

- Are you happy today?
- Are you feeling good this morning?
- Did you sleep well last night?
- Is there anything you want to go over?

Most of these types of questions can be answered with a simple 'yes' or 'no.' You might be able to question a little further, in some cases. However, it is best to stick with open-ended questions.

(Cesario, n.d.)

MORE TIPS FOR ASKING THE APPROPRIATE QUESTIONS

We have given you a few suggestions already for asking the appropriate questions, at the appropriate times, and in the appropriate ways. Basically, the questions need to be appropriate. After asking specific questions, you need to listen intently to what your client says and then ask good follow-up questions as needed. In this section, we will go over some crucial tips to help you understand how to ask the best questions in your coaching practice.

- Make your questions exploratory and experimental. Do not be harsh or direct with your questions, or your client can feel rushed and thrown off.
- Help your client when they need help in articulating their feelings. You are not telling them what their feelings are, but just clarifying them so you both understand.
- A question to ask in this instant could be: If that feeling you're describing could speak, what would it say?
- Help your client imagine their own success, and then plan from their perspective. The theory here is that it's easier to come up with solutions if a person imagines already being in the reality of the goal.
- Occasionally pause to help your client look more deeply within themselves. The question "what do you need to see here?" is used to help your client gain more insight into a current situation.
- Obtain evidence about what someone means. For instance, if they say that they want to be happy, what does that mean to them? What is their vision of happiness?
- Get your clients to keep themselves on track. It's not just about establishing goals, but implementing them too. As a coach, you don't tell your clients how to stay on track; they must decide that on their own.
- Find out what motivates your client. Literally ask them: What motivates you? This is a great way to get

to know your clients and what inspires them to keep moving forward.
- Help your clients help themselves. Do not carry the burden of their problems. Provide a safe space for them and ask in-depth, non-judgemental questions that will help them find solutions on their own.
- A good question to ask here is: How can you best support yourself right now?
- Find out what in a client's life cannot be taken away from them even if the worst happened. This does not have to be a material possession. It is usually something about their core values.
- Find a way for your clients to give themselves good advice. The client will know themselves best, so they will provide the best advice that will help their situation.
- Have your client imagine their ideal situation in the future and then ask them what advice their future self would give their present self.
- Determine what positive intention exists behind a destructive decision. Most individuals do things because they achieve some type of benefits from it. Even if it's something minor, it is enough to motivate them to keep moving.
- Determine your client's 'why.' Why do they want to do the things they do? What is whispering inside of them that is aching to come out? Don't just assume a client

will know the answers to these questions, and don't think that your 'why' is the same as theirs.
- Search for your client's deepest truths. Ask them directly what their truth is, and give them plenty of time to search for it.

As you practice your life coaching techniques, you will become much more familiar with how to ask the right questions. We advise that you practice on family and close friends before trying it on strangers. You can even practice by asking yourself some good questions. Just remember the core principles about asking the proper questions. Never make your client feel like they are rushed, and don't answer the questions for them. They need to come up with their own answers.

SOME MORE QUESTIONS

Like we said, asking questions is one of the most important aspects of life coaching. You will not have the answers for your clients. They will have the answers, and you just have to help find them. We will finish off this chapter by going over some of the best questions a life coach can ask during a session (Elsey, 2019).

- What would you like to have achieved by the end of this session? This is a great question to ask at the beginning of a coaching session so the client and coach are perfectly clear on what they're working on. This will bring great value to the session because it keeps everyone on track from the get-go.

- Out of everything you might have, what is one thing that is missing in your life right now? This question will help your client with determining unmet needs. You can also ask your client what they want more or less of in their lives.
- If there is anything you can change right now, what would it be? This is a great question to ask when a client is feeling overwhelmed and cannot get focused. This will help them remain grounded.
- How will you know when your desired goal has been achieved? Many people are not clear about their goals, so they never take action towards them. A question like this helps your client get more specific, so they know how to proceed.
- What is an initial step you can take right now? This question is great for larger goals. It will help a client get started. From here, you two can come up with further action steps that will move the client forward little by little. In this question, you can include steps to take over the next week, month, year, etc.
- What do you not want me to ask you? You can ask this question in a playful way, but it is really to get to know what areas of their life they are avoiding. You can stay

away from these areas at first and revisit them when the time is right.
- How does what you are doing serve you? This question can be directed at behavior that is self-sabotaging. This will help them take stock of how their current behavior patterns are either benefiting or hurting them. You can also ask the client what the benefit is of staying right where they are.
- How will you celebrate your victories? Celebrations are often overlooked, but they are a necessity during the growth process. Encouraging your clients to celebrate accomplishments will allow them to pause and take everything in. Otherwise, life will become a repetition of forgetful moments. In other words, stop and smell the roses once in a while.
- What areas of your life are not going well right now, and which ones are absolutely awesome? This is a great question to ask when your client is overly focused on making a great future but cannot focus on what's great now.
- What was the biggest win for you during the session today? Obviously, this question comes at the end and will help the client think about the benefits of coaching. As a coach, you will also understand what your clients get the most out of during a regular session.

Using the questions we went over in this chapter as an example, and come up with some of your own questions too. As you become more familiar with the process, you will be able to ask some very helpful questions that can be life-changing for your clients. Remember, even though these questions seem simple, many individuals never think about them deeply because they get so caught up in the craziness of life. You can assist them in becoming more grounded.

7

THE SCIENCE OF HABITS

How many times have you made a New Year's resolution, or heard somebody make one themselves, only to not follow through on it in any way? Or, they stuck to their new goals for a few days and then went back to their old ways? Some common resolutions people will make are to start eating healthy and going to the gym regularly. Unfortunately, they do not stick to these new goals. A common joke that's out there is to open a gym called 'Resolutions,' which turns into a bar after the first two weeks of January.

The point is, resolutions often fail because people are just motivating themselves through an arbitrary date on the calendar, but doing nothing to enforce new behavior in their lives. In order to follow through on these resolutions, these individuals must actively change their habits. Our habits are built up over time by practices we follow on a regular basis. To change these, we must alter our thought process and therefore adjust our behavior. Only then will we be able to follow through on our goals, whatever they may be.

HABITS AND THEIR FORMATION

A habit is defined as a regular tendency or practice that an individual has which is often hard to give up. People tend to develop strange tendencies as they grow older, which can be rooted in ideas that they learned as a child. For example, if a child's parents made them wake up every morning at five, that child will likely keep that routine until adulthood. It is what they are used to, and they have adapted both physically and mentally to this practice.

Habits can define us in many ways and also determine our future. There is a reason why some people perpetually succeed in life, while others always fall short. Some people lead healthy lives, while others suffer from chronic health issues. Some individuals always win, while others cannot catch a break. Yes, luck does play a role. However, if a person is always being dealt a bad hand, then continuously blaming it on misfortunes is just playing the victim card.

We are not denying that some people have it harder than others; however, everyone can still adjust their behaviors to improve their lives. The biggest problem that arises from bad lack is not poverty, poor health, or a lack of resources. Instead, it is the adaptation of bad habits, which are extremely hard to break.

Why Are Habits Difficult to Change?

According to Newton's Law of Motion, every object that is in a uniform state of motion tends to remain in that same state until some type of external force is applied to it. Of course, this external force does not have to be visible. For example, in the case of throwing an object into the air, gravity will only let it get so far before turning its trajectory back downwards. To summarize, objects in motion tend to stay in motion until something comes along to stop them.

The concept of the Law of Motion can also be attributed to human behavior, especially in regard to changing habits. Once a habit is developed, momentum takes over and the behavior keeps on going. The longer a person has had the habit, the more momentum it will have. The habits we develop go all the way down to our core and infiltrate every aspect of our being. This means we get a certain emotional and physiological response when we perform certain behaviors, and they make us feel good. Making that first shift is always the hardest part.

The difficulty in habit adjustment goes way beyond willpower. Our subconscious and unconscious minds, which are not immediately accessible in everyday life, are where habits form for the long term. This area of the mind is controlled by the basal ganglia in our brains. When we perform an action multiple times, it starts to get embedded in our brains. The actions we have been performing for years are so deeply embedded that they become a part of us, like an appendage. Therefore, it takes much less effort to repeat these activities than it does to engage in new ones.

Basically, to change a habit, we must force ourselves to do things on the conscious level, where we have immediate control, until our basal ganglia take over. At this point, our subconscious mind gets involved and a new habit starts forming. It really is a simple formula, but not easy in practice.

Think about habits as your brain's version of autopilot. Basically, you are performing tasks without even thinking about them. For routine activities, like getting ready for work or making breakfast, they can be a blessing. On the other hand, when we become comfortable, we start to develop bad habits without even realizing it. For example, instead of getting out of bed right away when the alarm goes off, we push the snooze button multiple times. Instead of making a healthy breakfast, we settle for a Pop-Tart and a sugar-filled coffee. Instead of going to bed at a reasonable time, we end up watching YouTube videos until midnight. Oh yeah, and don't forget about that late-night snack.

Bad habits are easier to slip into than good ones because they generally require less resistance. For instance, it is easier to sleep an extra hour every morning than it is to get up and exercise. It is easier to eat junk food because it often provides an immediate rush, rather than health food, which usually provides its benefits over the long run. The thirst for quick gratification is why negative habits are easier to form.

Let's Talk About Formation

Anybody that has tried to set a goal knows exactly how difficult it can be. Except for a few rare exceptions, changes do not occur overnight. It takes continuous effort and there will be many peaks and valleys along the way. Meaning, success never goes in a straight, upward trajectory.

When you are trying to make positive changes in your life, getting up and motivating yourself can become exhausting and drain all of your energy. If a person had to do this every day, being able to sustain it for the long run would be near impossible. This is where habit formation comes to our aid. While motivating yourself to make changes will be difficult for a while, as our new routines become ingrained into our subconscious minds, we will start performing them naturally.

For example, if you always hit the snooze alarm and wake up 30 minutes later than you plan, but want to change this, it will take time to get used to. On the first day, try waking up 10 minutes earlier than you used to. The next morning, go for 20 minutes. Finally, on the third day, wake up 30 minutes earlier than you're used to. From here, keep motivating yourself to wake up at this time. Day after day, it will become easier because your body and mind will become used to it. Eventually, waking up at the desired time will become natural, and you might not even need an alarm clock. Once you reach this state of habit formation, you are using much less energy to keep everything going.

Many experts believe that a habit takes about 21 days to form if focused on continuously. This is just an average and should not be taken as absolute gospel. However, you need to realize that a habit does take a while to form, so do not give up. If it's taking you longer than the average time, don't take it so hard. Everyone develops at their own pace, and it's important to remain consistent.

Let's go over some nuggets of wisdom related to habits. These will give you a better idea of how habits affect our lives, so they are easier to understand and manage.

Habits Emerge Without Our Consent

According to Charles Duhigg of *The Power of Habits* (The Coaching Academy Blog, n.d.) fame, the brain uses habits to help save energy to make important decisions. The brain will often implement what worked before in a certain situation, without our consent. In order to change this, we have to actively oppose it. As an example, if we come home from work every day and grab a soda from the fridge, our brain will know this every time and cause the same action to occur. If we are to change this activity, we must force ourselves to do something different. One day, we can reach for a healthy drink, like fresh juice or plain water. If we do this again for the next several days, our brain will start recognizing this pattern and start taking this step without our consent, until we decide to make another change.

Habit formation Has a Clear Pattern

The simple pattern for habit formation is a trigger, followed by a routine, followed by a reward. For instance, hunger can be the trigger, eating a snack can be the routine, and the feeling of being satiated can be the reward. The focal point here is the routine. What are you doing to satisfy the trigger, and what type of reward are you getting from the routine?

Think Small

This may sound confusing, but when it comes to habits, think small. When you are building a new habit, do not try to change everything at once. Instead, focus on small, repetitive steps that ultimately lead to big changes. If your plan is to begin an exercise routine, do not go to the gym on the first day and go crazy for an hour with the most insane workouts. All you have to do is feed your trigger, and it does not matter how long. So, on the first day, work out for five to 10 minutes, and increase the time from there. Put on those gym clothes every day and get to work. Whether you do 10 minutes or 30 minutes, you are creating a habit slowly.

Hone in on Your Triggers

This pattern provides a strong framework for building new habits with manageable steps. It allows you to focus on what is important to you and not become overwhelmed by major goals. Also, when you know that your bad habits start with a certain trigger, you can work on breaking these habits.

As an example, a heavy drinker may get into the habit of drinking several cans of beer at night while watching TV. In this case, watching TV is the trigger because it incites the person into having a few drinks. Once the individual realizes this, they can focus on changing their drinking habit by either replacing it with a new one or getting rid of the trigger.

Begin With the End in Mind

Before you break your goal down into smaller steps, visualize and understand what you want your end result to be. Think about your goal, and then break it down into manageable steps. Also, determine what smaller habits you need to develop to reach your objective. Will you need to learn a new skill, get some more training, or shift your mindset in some way? Take all of these into consideration and be as detailed as you can.

You Must Believe You Can Change

It can be easy to switch from a bad habit to a good one for a short-term period. However, to stick with it, you must have a belief in yourself that you can. If you don't believe in yourself, your new habits will fall apart quickly and you will relapse into your old routine.

It All Starts With a Good Start

There have been many schools of thought pointing to the fact that a good morning routine sets you up for a successful day ahead. There is plenty of anecdotal evidence to support this, as some of the most successful individuals in their field have a set morning ritual they adhere to. They wake up at a certain time, work out, eat a healthy breakfast, read, and plan for the day ahead. When they get their day started right, it sets a positive tone for the next several hours.

People like Jocko Willink, Tim Ferris, Oprah Winfrey, Barack Obama, and Tony Robbins work hard to win their mornings. Their devout morning routines help them gain focus, clarity, and energy to attack the day. For example, Tony Robbins does deep breathing exercises, followed by a cold shower. Oprah Winfrey performs meditation, followed by running on the treadmill to get her heart pumping (Adams, 2017).

What do you do every morning? If your routine is not inspiring and getting you ready to attack the day, you need to change quickly. Some examples of positive morning rituals include:

- Waking up early
- Exercising
- Reading
- Planning the day ahead
- Mindfulness practices
- Spending time with family

Author Amy Landino (The Coaching Academy Blog, n.d.) breaks down in her book *Good Morning, Good Life* how to successfully build habits for the morning that will set you up for a successful day. The key idea here is that the morning routine is not the actual goal, but the path towards the goal. It really doesn't matter what you do, as long as you can take time before the responsibilities of the day to reflect on yourself and your goals, and to take control of the day ahead. If you don't take time to focus on yourself, the day will rule you.

Choose the Habits You Want to Keep

Our daily routines often become cluttered with habits we don't especially enjoy or get anything out of. We just happened to develop them over time based on our experiences. This can lead to goals that we want nothing to do with. When we start focusing on habits that spark our joy, we can find more clarity on what type of life we actually want to live.

Habits Lead to Freedom

Many people believe that habits are too constraining. As a result, they become resistant to them. However, much of the literature provides a different perspective. Developing certain habits can provide you with more time, freedom, and energy for the things that are truly important to you.

For example, paying bills is never fun, but getting into the habit of paying them at a certain time every month can reduce stress and worry because it becomes natural. Eventually, you will sit down to pay your bills without even thinking about it. This will allow you to focus more on things you actually enjoy.

WHEN YOU'RE FINALLY READY TO MAKE A CHANGE

I don't want you to become disillusioned here. Changing habits can be difficult, but it is not impossible. If you follow specific strategies, you can begin altering your thought patterns, and eventually, your behavior. As a result, you will create significantly different outcomes. After changing your habits from negative to positive, you will finally start realizing why some people win and others lose. It is not limited to talent, skill, or genetic factors. The actions you commit to on a daily basis are what have the largest impact on your life. Therefore, the routine you develop is what determines the end goal.

The right time to start changing habits is when you decide to do so. Do not wait for an arbitrary date, like January 1st or another special occasion. When you are ready to make some changes, it's the right time to begin. If you want to start waking up early, do it tomorrow. Don't tell yourself you'll start after a week or after a certain moment in your life passes. These are just excuses, and you need to start nipping them in the bud.

As you go through changes, there will be many ups and downs, and plenty of mistakes will be made. This is okay because your goal is to take action and not to be perfect. Nobody is perfect, and trying to be is just a waste of time. Perfectionism makes you less productive because you are focused too heavily on something that is unattainable. Changing habits requires consistency, and some days you will be able to do more than others. As long as you are performing, you are progressing. If you exercise for 45 minutes one day and 30 minutes the next, don't be hard on yourself. At least you exercised consistently, which is the goal.

Finally, you must learn to embrace the power of triggers. They are what motivate you to perform a certain habit, whether good or bad. Focus on triggers that remind you to perform good habits, and ditch the ones that cause you to perform bad habits. If you are a regular smoker and love to light up when you're watching TV or hanging out at a bar, then you need to either modify these triggers or get rid of them completely. For example, while watching TV, you can sit in a different area of the room and you may not get the same cravings. If this doesn't work, figure out other ways to make changes.

Focus on triggers that result in positive attitudes. If you routinely go into the kitchen to grab a snack from a bowl, start filling that bowl with healthy fruits instead of candy. When you wake up in the morning, keep your phone away from you so you are not tempted to scroll through the first thing in the morning. Place a book on your nightstand so it is the first item you grab in the morning.

I will now go over some specific action steps to help change your bad habits. These strategies can work with whatever bad habit you are trying to change or replace. My advice to you is to focus on one habit at a time and prioritize with the most critical one. For example, if you have negative habits that are putting your health at risk, you may want to start with those and work your way down. Perhaps your money managing skills are poor and they are causing you to go into bankruptcy. Determine what areas in your life are harming you the most and go from there.

Acknowledge

Before you can fix a problem, you must recognize that it exists. Therefore, you must acknowledge a bad habit before you can start working on it. If you are in denial, you will get nowhere. I don't want you to think of yourself as weak. Bad habits exist for everyone, and it takes a lot of courage to admit to them. Once you wrap your head around your issues, it will become easier to manage them. It's similar to going into the hospital time and time again and not knowing why, but then finally getting a diagnosis. Even if it's kind of grim, actually knowing what you're dealing with will give you a fighting chance.

Acknowledging your bad habit is just like recognizing who your enemy is, and you will make a huge breakthrough by doing this. Give yourself credit for making it this far, because many people do not. Unfortunately, they live with the mindset that having any flaws is a bad thing, so they always deny doing anything wrong. This is just the first step, so let's keep going.

Understand

After acknowledging a bad habit, you must understand why you want or need to break it. This will become your ultimate reason. Is the bad habit causing you poor health, ruining your relationships, and negatively impacting your career? For example, you might be staying up late watching YouTube videos or eating a heavy meal right before going to bed, both of which are affecting your sleep patterns. Determine your reason for wanting to break free of your bad habits.

Habits are not limited to our actions, but also include our thoughts. If you constantly think negatively about any situation, that is a negative habit. Your emotional state can also be a trigger for other poor choices. For instance, when you're sad, you might overeat or drink excessively. When you are angry, you might start getting violent and breaking things. Focus on these cues and the relationship they have to your bad habits.

To fully understand your bad habits, you must step out of your comfort zone and have a full look at yourself from an outside perspective. Imagine sitting on a rooftop and watching yourself live your life. After acknowledging your bad habits and understanding why they exist, it will be easier to picture a different life for yourself. Okay, the first two steps of habit change are down. Now, we move onto the third step.

Shift

> "The speed of new habit pattern development is largely determined by the intensity of the emotion that accompanies the decision to begin acting in a particular way."
>
> — BRIAN TRACY

Our emotions that we carry with each habit will play a huge role in how quickly and intensely we reject bad habits and focus on the good ones. Both actions can be equally difficult. Since habits include both thoughts and actions, it is imperative to shift the way we think about and deal with our routines. If you want to start waking up early, not only do you have to perform the action of getting out of bed at a certain time, you must also have a positive way of thinking about it. If your thoughts revert to how tired you are and how miserable it will feel to leave your comfy bed, then it's a long shot that you will continue this habit for the long haul.

In addition to getting out of bed, you have to think about the benefits that come with it. For instance, getting out of bed earlier will allow you to get a good workout in, which will release endorphins to make you feel better. Also, getting out of bed early will give you more time to plan your day, eat a nutritious breakfast, and perform various other self-care activities. When you are shifting your habits, do it with your thoughts as well as your actions, and your chances of success will increase immensely.

When you transition the way you think, you are already programming your mind to know what it feels like to practice your new routines. In the case of working out in the morning, thinking about the endorphin release that will come out will allow your mind to already know what will happen post-exercise. When your mind and body are working in synchronicity, it is an amazing combination. Practice thinking only about positive outcomes to the point you will have no room to think about anything negative. Imagine your mind as a compartment with limited space. Why fill it with things that you don't want in there, like your negative thoughts? Clear those out, put new ones in, and never allow empty space for old thoughts to return. You will transition from bad habits to good habits in no time.

Visualize

It is now time to visualize a life filled with new, positive habits. Once you shift your focus to the benefits of forming new routines and rituals, it will be easy to picture your new life. This life will be filled with your positive habits and the abundance that comes with performing them. If your goal was to get up earlier every morning, visualize what your life will look like in the near future because of this action. Will you be in better shape because you exercised more and ate healthy meals? Will your career take off because you made more time to plan your day ahead? Finally, will your personal and familial relationships improve because you dedicated more time to them?

When you visualize, be very detailed in what you want to see. What time are you waking up and going to bed? Where are you working? What city, or even country, are you living in? How much energy are you feeling throughout the day? What emotions are running through your mind?

Practicing visualization allows you to get a head start on living your dream life. You need to visualize on a consistent basis. You can even make it part of your morning and nightly ritual. Doing it when you first wake up in the morning can motivate you into having a more productive day. You will realize that you are working towards this ideal life you have imagined. Not only will training your mind to see what your new habits will bring you to make it easier to stick with them, but your mind will also think you are already there.

Reward

Okay, you are done now, so let's party! No, I am just kidding. In all seriousness, though, habit formation is not easy. It will take a lot of time, effort, and discipline on your part. You should be proud of the milestones you accomplish, so take the time to reward yourself along the way. Do not go overboard and fall off the wagon, but definitely perform acts that are rewarding to you. For example, if you have started a healthier meal plan and have been executing it for several weeks, then give yourself a cheat meal, or even cheat day. Just don't allow it to turn into several cheat days or weeks. Also, give yourself a pat on the back regularly. Sit down in a quiet space and think about what you have already accomplished.

Embrace your new changes that developed from healthier habits. Use these changes to inspire you to keep moving forward. Think about life as a constant learning and growing experience. You will never become perfect, so there are always areas you can improve upon. Out with the old and in with the new, as the old adage states.

WHAT'S IN A DAY? OR 21?

Every one of us grows at a different pace. Depending on the individuals, it can take anywhere from a few days to several weeks, or even months, to officially form a new habit. However, many experts believe that 21 days is the average amount of time it takes. The number was first referenced by Dr. Maxwell Maltz (Clear, 2018) who was an American cosmetic surgeon, and author of the book *Psycho-Cybernetics.* He noticed in his patients that it took about 21 days for them to come to terms with their new image after an extensive procedure. This was more of a situational observation by Dr. Maltz, and not really an in-depth study.

As his book became more popular, so did the 21-day theory. Several experts began tying it to habit formation, and it began getting known as factual. All we can say is that you can use this 21-day model as a guide, but don't take it as gospel. What you can do is expect to follow a certain routine for a minimum of 21 days, or three weeks, before it becomes natural to you. Once again, don't just assume this will be the case. Don't be discouraged if you are at the 21-day mark and don't feel like your new habit has formed. In addition, do not just slack off after the three-week period. Your new habit should be a lifelong transformation and not just a quick fix.

HOW A LIFE COACH CAN HELP WITH HABIT CHANGE

If you decide to pursue a career in life coaching, a large portion of your time will be spent helping your clients with habit changes. As their coach, you can be there as a guide and they will have to come to their own realizations. You can also be the outside perspective they need. People often cannot see the forest through the trees, which means they are way too closed off within themselves to see what issues they have going on.

During the first step of habit change, the coach can assist their client in recognizing the negative areas of their life and what might be causing them. From here, they can come in contact with their bad habits. After this, they can acknowledge their existence. The coach can help ease their anxiety by letting them know it takes strength to admit faults.

After helping your client acknowledge their poor habits, assist them in understanding what negative effects they are causing. The client will start seeing how much of an impact their routines have on their outcomes, and this can inspire them to make some changes. Once again, let your client know they are doing the right thing and are not weak for recognizing areas where they need improvement.

Now, you can help your client come up with strategies to make adjustments. Give them the tools to start thinking about the positive aspects of new habit formations. Also, help them start visualizing. You can use a few minutes during your session to help them come up with a picture-perfect life. You will notice a major change in their mindset and actions.

Of course, you need to hold your client accountable too because it is ultimately up to them. They need to do the work; you are just there to provide support. When you see progress, provide encouragement and congratulate them on their accomplishments. Provide some instructions on how they can reward themselves for reaching personal milestones.

As a life coach, you can help your client improve their career, social life, health, relationships, and so much more by guiding them in changing their habits. Not everyone can do it on their own. However, everyone has the power to do so, but just needs a little direction. This is where true life coaching comes into play.

Never discount the power of rituals. Think of each habit you possess as a building block of a large structure. If one of the building blocks is dysfunctional, the structure might lean. If there are enough dysfunctional building blocks, then the structure might fall over altogether. Your goal should be to eliminate as many negative building blocks in the structure or your life so that you do not fall apart. Good luck on your habit formation journey!

PROMOTING A HABIT CHALLENGE

A great way to help your client develop a new habit and hold them accountable at the same time is to promote a habit challenge. This is where you challenge them to come up with a habit they want to change or form, and then give them a certain time limit to follow through on it. Now, this deadline is not meant for the full development of the new habit. As we said, everyone works on their own timeline. However, this can push them to stay on track with their goals and make serious improvements in their lives.

To begin, pick an arbitrary number like 21, 25, or 30. This is the number of days your client is required to follow through on their chosen ritual. For example, if it is to exercise for at least 15 minutes every morning, the challenge is to do this for the set number of days straight. So, if the decided number is 30, your client will have to exercise 15 minutes every day for 30 days straight, rain or shine.

After the 30 days, assess your client and ask how easy they find their new routine. If they feel like it's natural and they can do it easily, you can use this same challenge for other habits. See for yourself how this method works.

8

THE MINDSET COACHING

Think about your mind as a set of pathways that are built over time. The building blocks are our thoughts and actions. When we repeat these thoughts and actions continuously, they further cement the pathways for us. After a while, these avenues in our minds are completely set. Therefore, it becomes effortless to think and do the same things over and over again. We create a natural pattern that flows like an electrical current through wires. In order to change these wires, we have to actively restructure them. We literally must take them down and rebuild them in a different order. After this, our thoughts and actions will be vastly different.

For instance, people tend to believe negative thoughts because it takes less of a struggle than thinking positively. As a result, they become natural for us, and our minds automatically revert to this way of thinking without allowing a positive thought to enter. This becomes our mindset, and we are stuck with it until we decide to do something about it. This is where a certain type of life coaching comes into play: the mindset coach.

A mindset coach can help to rewire an individual's mindset so they can start realizing their full potential. After working with a mindset coach, people end up becoming the best versions of themselves. Mainly, they start believing in themselves. Like any other type of life coach, they avoid giving direct advice, and rather guide their clients in finding their own answers.

Right now, you might be wondering how all of this occurs. The process is actually simple, but it will take effort on everyone's part. It involves preparing an individual to develop a thought process that is solid and geared towards a better life. This new thought process will help them embrace changes and make difficulties in their life appear like a cakewalk.

After working with a mindset coach, a client will feel a significant boost in their energy. People underestimate just how much their way of thinking affects their energy levels and productivity. However, negative thinking drains our energy and can mentally paralyze us into accomplishing nothing. A mindset coach will help develop more willpower in their clients, and therefore make them more optimistic about their circumstances.

The real change that occurs happens from within a client, where the best answers come from. This is why a mindset coach will heavily promote self-efficacy. As such, the coach must let their clients know they are capable of doing extraordinary things. Remember that people who succeed at the highest level were once ordinary people who did extraordinary things.

Throughout history, many people have risen from the ashes in some of the worst conditions anyone can know and created an abundance for themselves that most people cannot even imagine. They had it within them to make significant changes, not because they have superpowers, but a super will. If they can do it, so can you. One of the things you have to start doing is something we have promoted excessively in this book, and that's imagining. Use your imagination, just like when you were a kid.

YOU ARE HERE TO DO EXTRAORDINARY THINGS

Yes, a mindset coach can help their clients in many aspects of their lives. They guide people in so many ways. For example, the client might be going through a major career change. This could be changing job titles, changing companies, coming back to work after getting laid off, or even starting a business. The mindset coach can assist them in taking the first step, which is often the most crucial one. Once a client gets started, the mindset coach can continue to provide guidance and encouragement through all of the difficult moments. Sometimes, having a cheerleader in your corner is essential—someone who will believe in you enough to hold you accountable.

A mindset coach can also help people with changes in their lifestyle. A person might be transitioning to new surroundings, whether it's a new house, town, or even a new country altogether. This can also relate to new work environments that come with a career change. Change is very scary and uncomfortable, no matter who you are. Even if the change is necessary, a lot of uncertainty can come with it. Uncertainty can become crippling for people, especially if they are not used to it. A mindset coach can help provide some clarity during moments of mass confusion. They will guide an individual on how to enjoy and embrace their new lifestyle. They can even help clients realize their new situation is better than their old one. After this, it's out with the old and in with the new.

Sometimes, people feel stuck and don't know where to go. There can be many reasons for this or no reason at all. They are just in a position they don't want to be in and can't figure out how to get out of it. All of us fall into a rut, and it can be very frustrating and even depressing. It's like falling into a shallow pit, where you can see the light, but have no idea how to climb out. A mindset coach can help with the transition process in this type of scenario. They can revive someone's energy and help them to thrive by providing encouragement and an outside perspective. Sometimes, people just need a little nudge, and the mindset coach can give it to them.

A mindset coach can help clear all of the noise that exists in the world. Sometimes, the answers are there, but it's too loud to hear them. You need to block out that noise to stay focused. After working with a mindset coach, people will start to realize their true purpose in the world. Despite all of the craziness, every individual plays a valuable role in the world, and we must never forget that.

"None can destroy iron, but its own rust can! Likewise, none can destroy a person, but its own mindset can."

— RATAN TATA

Iron is one of the most durable materials on the planet. It is powerful enough to build train tracks and versatile enough to make amazing products. A train track made of iron can have countless trains running across it for years and years and still hold its original strength. You can burn it, freeze it, or throw it into the ocean, and it will still remain iron. However, when the rust builds up long enough, the piece of iron begins to rot and will eventually destroy itself. To prevent this from happening, the rust needs to be cleared on a regular basis.

The same concept applies to our mindset. Think of your mindset as a piece of iron. Now, picture everything in your surroundings, like insults, criticisms, failures, and losses, as the rust that is trying to destroy you, as all of the environmental factors try to destroy the iron. They won't destroy you, but they can alter your mindset towards the negative, which will ultimately bring you down if you don't clear all of it out. Once again, this is where the skills of a mindset coach come into play. They will help remove the metaphorical rust from your life.

WHO CAN USE A MINDSET COACH?

The short answer is everyone. A mindset coach can help a person in many different situations in life, including career, health, and relationships. Our mindset impacts every area of our lives and if we want to be successful, we must have the right thought processes. If you don't believe you can accomplish something, then you won't. It's as simple as that.

Now, will failures still occur? They definitely will. However, the great thing about having a positive mindset is that it gives you the strength, endurance, and clarity to keep charging through the low points in your life. With a negative mindset, a person sees no hope and simply gives up. Furthermore, a mindset coach will help lift a person up when they do fall down and make sure they keep that positive mindset.

After hearing about all the ways a mindset coach can help someone, are you ready to go down this path? We hope so, because it is a great avenue to make real changes in a person's life. You can also make a great living for yourself, as long as you know who to sell your services to. A large part of the coaching business is marketing since this is how you will ultimately obtain your clients. Even if you are the best coach in the world, if nobody knows about you, then you will ultimately get nowhere.

Now, let's return to the original question of this section: Who needs a mindset coach? Rather than bore you with too many details, we will provide some anecdotes to help clarify where and when a mindset coach can come in.

- Mike is a senior vice president of a major corporation. While he has had much career success in the past, he is currently going through a crisis. It is weighing down on him heavily and he cannot perform well. As more time passes, he is becoming less motivated.
- Mike can definitely use a mindset coach in this example. The coach will help him understand what is creating issues in his life and help find ways to move forward.
- Jenny has achieved high levels of success in her career. The sky's the limit for her, but she needs some extra motivation to reach her next promotion.
- A mindset coach can help Jenny dig deep down to find her motivation and give her the extra boost she needs.
- Benny is a new entrepreneur with a great idea. However, he does not know how to proceed forward with his venture, plus he needs a lot of self-improvement in his personal life.
- A mindset coach can determine what areas Benny

needs the most help in and then assist him in taking the first steps towards building his enterprise.
- Kenneth is a very successful salesperson. In fact, he could literally be the poster child for sales. Recently, his sales have been going down and he cannot figure out why. He is getting depressed and anxious and no longer knows what to do.
- A mindset coach can help Kenneth determine what changes have been made and why his sales have been going down. From here, they can both figure out if it's something Kenneth can control, and how.

These are just a few examples, and we can come up with many more. Think about some situations in your own life where you could have used a mindset coach. We are sure that you can find plenty. Also, think about people who have been through many struggles and just needed someone to guide them. All of these individuals, and others like them, are your potential customers.

HOW DOES A MINDSET COACH HELP?

We will now get into some specific strategies that a mindset coach can use to help. Also, remember that the skills and techniques discussed in the earlier chapters can apply here too. When you become aware of the many benefits of mindset coaching, you can educate your potential clients about them too.

So, let's go over some ways a mindset catch can help those who need them.

Building Self-Awareness

People will turn to their family and friends to learn more about themselves. They will ask them what they think and how they should behave. Furthermore, they will let people tell them what to do with their lives. Taking this a step further, people will rely on the opinions of neighbors, coworkers, acquaintances, and even total strangers to learn about who they are. The major problem here is that these individuals will come from an area of complete bias. They will not come from an objective viewpoint. Even if they don't have a bias, they will make other blunders like giving out lectures or directly telling people what to do.

In order to gain self-awareness, people must find a different perspective. A mindset coach is a perfect individual for this. A mindset coach will tell someone what they need to hear and not what they want to hear while coming from a place of total objectivity.

As a mindset coach, it will be your job to provide a clear-cut reflection of a client's weaknesses. You will also highlight their strengths, so they know precisely where they stand. This will give them an honest picture of who they are and increase their self-awareness. In turn, they will become more accountable for their situation.

Self-awareness will provide a major boost in motivation. As a result, these self-aware people will seek out healthier relationships, and this will provide them with an even more positive environment. These benefits of self-awareness also lead to higher productivity and much more vibrant life.

Through all of these changes, a person will develop a healthier mindset and a reduction in stress and anxiety. Building self-awareness is vital for self-growth.

Creating Accountability

As a mindset coach, you will come into contact with clients who lack responsibility. They ignore their duties in life and seem to have no determination. As a result, life seems to be passing them by. Why do they act in this manner? Because they have no accountability and take no responsibility for their lives. These individuals often become perpetual victims in society who blame everyone else for their issues. By being their coach, you will help change their mindset, so they start having accountability for their own lives.

Accountability is a necessity for a strong mindset. A mindset coach needs to be honest with their clients and let them know they own the responsibility for their actions. Whether the results are good or bad, they own them. Once the client realizes this, they will start making more rational decisions because they know the heat will fall on them ultimately.

Of course, all of this is easier said than done. Building accountability takes a while. It will not happen overnight or with one good pep talk. If a person has been avoiding responsibility all their lives, it will take time for them to come to terms with being accountable. Building accountability takes a lot of motivation, which we will discuss in the next section.

Increasing Motivation

This goes beyond opening a book of motivational quotes and regurgitating them all. At most, these will provide short-term motivation that will likely dissipate after one session. The goal is to rewire the mind and change the way a client thinks. This will lead to results that are authentic and sustainable. The client must determine their own hows and why of living their life.

As a mindset coach, you must make a client find their inner drive. From here, they will learn to thrive, and not just survive, in their work and life. Help them discover their intrinsic values and even modify them if needed. The ultimate goal here is to help your clients become someone who always gets results. They will live up to their real potential.

Setting Realistic Goals

Without solid goals, we would all be wandering aimlessly through life. Unless that is somehow a person's goal, they have some work to do. Goal setting does not come easy to many people and there can be many reasons for it, like being unmotivated or overwhelmed, underestimating themselves, or being stuck in a dilemma. They may also be too close to a situation to determine if a goal is achievable or not.

A mindset coach will make the goal-setting journey more manageable. The coach will guide someone towards the right path while this client determines their true goals. As they both go along, the coach will ensure their client remains on the correct path to prevent their mind from wandering all over the place. When an individual is focused, they have a better chance of achieving their selected goals.

An increased focus will lead to a stronger mindset. From here, they will be able to avoid distractions.

Boosting Self-Reflection

People fail to reflect on their lives. This is why so many people do not learn from their mistakes. They do not perform an honest reflection of their successes and failures to see where they can improve in the future. Life is a constant process of struggle, and when a person is able to overcome, that is when success is achieved. The mindset coach can help a client reflect on their goals, as well as the journey to get there.

After a client achieves their desired goals, the coach can help draft new ones. When one mountain has been climbed, another one still exists. Life is a constant journey of self-improvement, and a mindset coach plays a big role in this.

With all of these benefits of mindset coaching, it won't be difficult to convince clients that they need your help. At least, not the ones who are willing to change. You can help them in this process, as well, but in the end, they will decide when you are needed.

THE END OF A SESSION

You need to make sure every session you go through with a client is valuable. While you will make more breakthroughs on some days way more than others, you want to make progress every day. This is an hour that you and your client will never get back. Furthermore, an excellent session can turn into an excellent week, month, or year, etc. Avoid getting frustrated because even a little progress is still progress.

To summarize, the following are some of the objectives you should aim to achieve with your coaching sessions. It may take a bit of time, but as long as you are moving in the right direction, that is what matters most.

- Clarity so they are not hiding from the truth.
- A mindset that claims the client's true desires.
- A clear vision that is exciting for your client. Fear, stress, and anxiety will slowly vanquish.
- Transformation tools that your client can use every day. Remember, what your clients do outside of the

sessions are just as important as the sessions themselves.
- Realization of their self-worth.
- Overcoming procrastination and resistance to change.
- Focusing on the positive without complaining. No more making excuses.
- Having clarity on goals.
- Development of consistent habits to get closer to dreams.
- Feeling motivated, having fun, being inspired, and showing confidence.
- Being able to visualize the big picture.
- Allowing your thoughts to roam free and no longer be locked in a cage—essentially, not living with limitations.

9

BUSINESS COACHING

So, you are finally tired of working for a boss that does not appreciate you or pay you fairly for your labor. You decide to leave and start your own business. Congratulations! You became inspired by all of the entrepreneurs around you who made their own way and built a sustainable enterprise. Whether it's the large corporation downtown, your favorite restaurant to frequent on weekends, or the laundromat around the corner, someone worked hard to open these businesses to provide a service for the general public.

With the advent of the internet and the constant improvements in technology, online and remote business ventures have also sprouted up. In fact, these have become more profitable and practical than old school brick-and-mortar shops of the past. Many physical businesses are even transitioning to remote and online functionalities. These changes have resulted in many more entrepreneurs sprouting up, leading to more financially independent people. On the flip side, it has led to more business failures, as well.

There are many misconceptions out there about business. This is because people see the end results, and not all of the struggles that happened beforehand. In addition, they do not realize the issues that continue to exist for business owners, many of whom are hanging on by a thread. When these individuals become inspired, they move forward without much preparation. Maybe they received advice from a few business owners, read a few books, and attended some seminars, but they did not do all of the necessary legwork to help make the business sustainable. This is why so many businesses close their doors within the first year.

Before a person even considers opening a business of any kind, they must do proper research, including market trends, how they can help the public, marketing options, budgeting, and of course, a business plan. There are many moving parts, so it can be impossible to take everything into account. If someone is lucky, they can find a business mentor to guide them. Others look towards family and friends for advice, but as we have established already, they are not the most reliable source for unbiased information. In fact, many of them may try to talk you out of it and stay on the safe route. The last thing you want when trying to start a business is for someone to take away your motivation.

Another great option is to hire a business coach. A business coach typically has a background in business and uses their knowledge and experience to guide others in their entrepreneurial ventures. While there is plenty of information online and a wealth of business books available, it is all very generic and not targeted towards your specific business, which will have its own challenges.

Business coaches are able to provide a more personalized approach, which many future business owners will benefit from. In addition, they can hold people accountable for performing the necessary steps and not taking shortcuts. While people can read about the action steps they need to perform, it does not mean they will do them. It is human nature to find an easier way, and this will lead to skipping over critical tasks. Suddenly, the easier way turns into the hard way. A business coach can help ensure their clients stay on track and don't try to skip ahead.

A business coach will work alongside their clients through every process they are needed. This includes the planning phase, startup, and actually running the business. Once again, a business coach will not give direct answers or advice, but will help a business person navigate through rough waters in order to find their own solutions. Just like if you're on a sports team, you will have someone in your corner. This will lead to less stress and worry, which is a priceless benefit in and of itself.

YOU AS A BUSINESS COACH

If you have a background in business and want to enter the life coaching field, business coaching might be right up your alley. If you do not have a business background yet, you can develop these skills as a general life coach and then transition into business coaching. While you are growing your life coaching clients, you will learn several strategies and techniques of entrepreneurship, and these will serve you very well.

The focus of this section will be to discuss your role as a business coach and how you can help your clients with their success. You will serve as both a trainer and a mentor. You will be by your client's side to serve as a valuable source for information. Your clients will need help refining their talents, assessing and narrowing their goals, guiding their decisions, big and small, and doing whatever is needed to help their business succeed.

Right from the start, whenever your client hires you, your role will be as a guiding light every step of the way. The best-case scenario is that your client hires you at the beginning, from the moment they think about starting a business. That way, you can help them with the whole pre-planning, initiation, growth, and continued success phases.

At the start, you must learn everything you can about your client's company so that you are going in without any major surprises. Understand the value of the brand, the target customers, and the many challenges they are facing and will run into down the line. Whatever information you can gather will make your job much easier.

Once you have learned what the company has to offer, it's time to learn about their vision. What do they see for themselves in the future, including short- and long-term goals? Are they expecting to grow the company, or keep it a small operation? Make sure you get clear goals from your client. If they don't have any, you need to sit down with them and figure out what they are.

Every business owner will have a unique vision for their company. This is where business coaching can become more valuable than any book or seminar. You will be able to provide personalized attention based on the vision your client has.

After having all of this initial information, you can now help your client come up with beneficial and attainable goals. Take into account their current finances, time availability, motivation, and other resources. These goals will ultimately work towards fulfilling the vision that was created earlier. Once these goals are set, then it's time to take action. You will assist your client in meeting their desired goals by coming up with a set of strategies and action steps. These strategies will also help navigate through challenges and unforeseen circumstances.

Running a business, whether small or large, is risky, challenging, and nerve-racking. Just knowing that a strong and informative support system exists will put your client at extreme ease.

As you can see, business coaches are not just there for struggling businesses. They can be the key to pushing an already successful business to the next level or helping a new business grow and prosper as seamlessly as possible.

SELLING YOURSELF AS A BUSINESS COACH

Business owners, entrepreneurs, CEOs, and other business professionals may be some of the hardest people to sell to. New or prospective business owners will be squeezing every penny and will not want to hire a coach that will cost more of an investment. CEOs and other heads of large corporations are highly suspicious of people they don't know and might be resistant to your coaching services. They will probably not see the value at first.

As a business coach, it is your job to show others that you are valuable. On top of having a good marketing strategy, you have to show your potential clients that the benefits you provide will heavily outweigh the cost to hire you. Even though that's your goal, they may not know that. They may see you as a swindler.

When you are pitching your services, you will need to provide the many benefits of working with a life coach. The following are some of the best reasons to give them.

Taking More, Better, and Smarter Actions

People will do exactly what they want to do in the end. A business coach will be able to work with a client to determine exactly what they want for themselves and their business. Once a business person creates an ideal goal, they are much more likely to take consistent action to reach it. In essence, they will be taking more, better, and smarter actions because they have a goal they truly want. Having clear goals in business is imperative; otherwise, you will have no idea when your business is succeeding or failing.

Having a More Balanced Life

Having it all means that you have a balanced life. This can be very difficult to achieve because a business does take up so much of your time. A businessperson must learn to be selfish. This is different from egotistical. A good business coach will show their clients exactly how to be selfish, yet still responsible, so they get their needs met and are still liked by people. The client will design their ideal life of balance between business, home, health, and self-care.

Keeping and Making More Money

Of course, the main reason to go into business is to make a profit. The money is where it's at. You deserve to keep more of your money because you worked hard to build your business. A business coach will help you set up a plan to bring in more profits. In addition, they will help you with a financial plan and help design a strategy to earn more from your business. You will also get more customers. This benefit alone will be worth the investment in a business coach. As a coach yourself, you should probably provide a summary of how you can help the client's business thrive.

They Will Reach for More

A business coach is a partner. When someone has a partner they trust, they will reach for more because they can afford to. While reaching for more, the business person will not be consumed in the process.

Make Better Decisions Due to Better Focus

A good business coach knows the value of sharing ideas with someone who understands them. They are subjective enough to want more for their clients, but objective enough to not be biased in their approach. At the very least, a business coach can be an unbiased listening ear who can hear what their client has to say. Sometimes, just talking to someone who doesn't show judgment is enough to make ideas become more clear.

Having More Sustainable Energy

When a business person has fewer problems and more solutions, they will have more energy too. This will increase their productivity and outcomes, as well. When working with a coach, the business owner will also know they have a backup.

THE BIGGEST OBSTACLES FOR SUCCESSFUL BUSINESS COACHING

As a business coach, you will be an entrepreneur yourself. You will need to market, set up a business plan, watch your finances, pay taxes, and deal with the other challenges that come with running a business. This field of coaching is very rewarding, but it also comes with its share of obstacles. If you want to become successful in this field, you must be aware of these challenges and how to overcome them. The following list was from a survey done on those who wanted to become business coaches in the future.

Lack of Confidence/Fear of Failure

Lack of confidence was the number one response that individuals give as their biggest obstacle towards becoming a successful business coach. Many were concerned when it came to coaching high-level executives. They worried about how they could pull it off and not look like a fraud. They also wondered what would happen if they were put in this situation and they failed. Would their coaching business come to a screeching halt?

One thing to understand is that being a business coach does not mean you know the ins and outs of every business. That would be impossible. Being a business coach involves having the right coaching strategies and the ability to ask thoughtful and purposeful questions. This means that your coach training is essential for helping you develop your techniques and style so you can help other people in their circumstances.

Remember one more thing: As the coach, you are not giving any business professionals the answers. They are coming up with their own solutions. Your role is to guide them as needed. So, don't worry that you are not as experienced as the high-level executive at a Fortune 500 company or that you haven't owned a restaurant for 20 years. Running the business is their role; coaching is yours.

Finally, you are a business owner as a life coach. You had to develop specific strategies, and if they are good enough to attract major clients, you must be doing something right. Use these wins as inspiration. You can definitely handle it.

Lack of Business Skills

I addressed this a little bit in the previous section, but many inspiring coaches feel like they don't have adequate business skills. Here are some of the concerns:

- Whether the business experience they have is relevant or not.

- They know how to succeed themselves, but are unsure if they can coach others to do the same.
- They fear their lack of knowledge in areas of sales, finance, the tech industry, or any other field they might come across.

Well, it's good that you are a little worried. This shows that you care about helping others and are not overconfident. The solution here is to appreciate the integrity you possess and make sure to never lose it. Here are a few more things to consider:

- You will learn how relevant your business skills are once you start coaching clients.
- Coach training will show you how to coach others. Your goal is not to learn about every industry that exists in the world. Your goal is to learn how to coach anyone from any industry in the world.
- Coaching skills like communication, team-building, controlling emotions, and asking appropriate questions can be applied to any context.

The issue of lacking business skills will begin to resolve when you start moving forward. Don't allow this fear to stop you because many business owners can benefit from your skillset.

Lack of Resources

Resources generally refer to time and proper connections. Money can cover the costs of a startup. If you don't have certain skills, like website design, then you can hire someone to do it for you. If you have the right connections, you can find clients much more easily. All of this is true. You do need some money and connections to build a new business, including a coaching business.

How much do you need? Surprisingly, not very much. The most important aspect of a coaching practice is the message that you bring. This will heavily make up for any lack of resources you have. Pay more attention to sending out the right message than having a lack of proper resources. Those can definitely be gained.

Time Management

Time management is definitely a crucial element in starting any business. Time is something you will never get back, so you must use it wisely. A common misconception related to time is how long it takes to get things done. Becoming a full-fledged business coach from start to finish can take a long time. This is especially true when you take into account marketing and building up your clientele. Don't believe that you will start training tomorrow and then have a successful practice within a couple of weeks. It does not work that way.

I want you to consider something. The time will pass anyway, so use it to build up your skills and business load. If you stick with it, you will make continuous progress and still become a business coach in a reasonable amount of time. Set timelines for yourself to complete certain milestones. For example, you will have gone through coach training within one month from now, have a functioning website a week after the training is complete, and begin marketing the following week. Stick to these timelines as much as possible.

Procrastination

Who doesn't procrastinate these days? Way too many people do, and this is the enemy of productivity. If you procrastinate when trying to build up your coaching practice, you will deny yourself the success you can obtain. In some cases, it can ruin your business as a whole. Imagine having clients and not attending to their needs because you are procrastinating. Your clients won't appreciate it, and you will not develop a good name. We suggest setting up a weekly calendar of goals you want to achieve and sticking to them religiously. In addition, take some training on overcoming procrastination if you feel this is an issue for you.

When work needs to get done, start on it as soon as possible. If something is due in five days, work on it daily so you are not overly stressed and rushing on the fifth day. When you are rushed, simple errors get made, and they add up to be a lot.

All of these obstacles can be overcome. Never let them, or any others, stop you from living your dream as a business coach.

BUILDING TRUST

We have spoken throughout this book about the need to build trust. A relationship between a coach and their client is all about trust. If it does not exist, progress will never be made. A client will never open up about their issues, and the interaction will become pointless.

No matter what type of business you are in, your client and customers must have faith that you have their best interest at heart. They cannot feel like you're taking advantage of them in some way. It certainly cannot come across like you want to take their money. Remember, building trust can take a while and be lost in an instant. However, when you build trust, it will pay off immensely.

Life coaching is all about building trust and this section will go over some habits that will help you earn it. The key word is 'earn.'

Figure Out What Integrity Means to You

Believe it or not, not everyone agrees on what's right or wrong. We have the major issues that are accepted across the board, like it's wrong to kill, steal, or intentionally harm others. Even with these, you can get into some gray areas where people will disagree. You must determine what your core values are and stick to them. One of these values should be integrity, which means being honest and having strong moral principles. Your integrity must guide every interaction you have with a client. Check in with yourself every day and determine if you are conducting yourself with honesty and have the client's best intentions in mind.

Give Your Clients Peace of Mind

Your clients should always feel like you are taking good care of them. You don't have to be perfect, but you should always give everything you have. Despite how you are feeling, you should give your clients the best service you can. They rely on you and deserve the best of you.

Truthfully, if you are in a coaching session and your mind is wandering, you are doing your clients a huge disservice. They are there to have you listen to them, and you are there to help them find solutions. No matter what is going on, show up and give it your all.

Keep Your Word

You're probably saying 'duh,' but this is something that must be addressed. If you make a promise, then keep it. Clients have come to expect a lack of follow-through from many businesses today. Do not allow this to happen in your coaching practice. You are dealing with people in some of their most vulnerable times, and they rely on you to keep your word.

This goes for small promises, as well. Don't ever assume that because the promise you made was insignificant, you can just not follow up on it. First of all, it might be significant to your client, and they will resent you for not taking it seriously. Second, if you break a promise, it will slowly become a habit. So, don't ever start.

Schedule Some Time for Nurturing

Schedule a little additional time when you can to further develop a client relationship. Meet somewhere outside of a regular coaching session. For example, meet up for coffee, have an extra phone conversation, or buy them a small gift. It doesn't have to be anything lavish. Just let them know you value the coach-client relationship. Make them feel special. This will provide them more encouragement to follow through on action steps.

Be Upfront With Them About What You Offer

The client must have a clear understanding of what services you actually provide. Never advertise a service you cannot deliver on. If you feel you cannot offer the client what they need, like therapy or more advanced techniques you are not trained for, then be upfront with them. They will always appreciate your honesty.

Keep Things Consistent

Your clients will always expect the best level of care, so give it to them. Make sure you are living up to your commitment with each interaction.

Don't Fake Authenticity

Clients will be able to see through a facade. Maybe not right away, but eventually, they will. You cannot fake authenticity. You must genuinely care for your clients and want to help them. Let your real personality shine through and allow them to fall in love with it. As a coach, you are selling yourself too, after all.

Face-to-Face When You Can

We realize you will have clients from all over the world. Also, there will be many other reasons why face-to-face interactions will not always be possible. However, when they are, make it happen. This will allow for a stronger connection between a coach and client. Furthermore, if you are doing a remote session, opt for a video call over a regular phone call.

Don't Abandon Your Clients for New Ones

As you gain more clients when your business begins to thrive, do not sacrifice the service you have been giving to your old clients. They have been loyal and still rely on your help. Never abandon them for new clients. If you ever get to the point where you are too overwhelmed, then avoid bringing in anyone new until you can get more settled.

When You Mess Up, Own It and Fix It

When you screw something up, will you feel foolish? Probably. Will you look foolish? Most likely. Do you know what's worse than being a screw-up? Being a liar. Therefore, when you make a mistake, own it and fix it. Don't try to hide it. We are all humans and make mistakes. Your clients will appreciate your honesty more than they care about you messing up. Just make sure you are not making the same mistakes over and over again.

You are on your way to becoming a highly successful business coach. If this area does not tickle your fancy, other coaching options exist too.

CONCLUSION

All of us at Elvin Coaches want to thank you for taking the time to read our book, *Don't Make Me Use My Life Coach Voice*. We hope that it painted a detailed portrait of what a life coach is and the value they can bring to the people who need them. Life coaching is definitely a growing field with many different offshoots. Every type of coaching subset has its own unique methods that work for them. For example, intuitive coaching, mindset coaching, and business coaching, all of which we covered, can benefit from their separate techniques. At the same time, the core principles of the coaching field can be used across the spectrum.

As we went through the different parts of the book, we provided the foundations of what life coaching is, the benefits the practice provides, common misconceptions, and reasons why you, the reader, should consider this as a profession. While the monetary gains can be abundant once you become good at your craft, the true value in life coaching rests in how many people from all walks of life can be touched by your special gifts. Literally anyone can benefit from life coaching, which was demonstrated by the number of different styles and techniques we went over, plus the variety of high-profile individuals who have used and praised life coaches.

Habit formation is another main topic that was covered in this book. Improving your circumstances is all about changing your habits, or daily routines and rituals. What you think and do on a daily basis determines the outcomes you will ultimately get. Therefore, a major focus of any coach-client relationship needs to be that of creating and reforming habits. When a client learns these techniques, they can positively change any area of their lives.

A life coach can literally help a person in every aspect of their life, including career, health, spirituality, and relationships. Some coaches choose to become specialized, while others stay more general. One thing a life coach is not, no matter what kind, is a therapist. They do not deal with mental health disorders, or anything of that nature. Their goal is to focus on the present and build towards a better future for their clients.

Another foundational principle with life coaching is that they don't give people answers. They are more focused on asking the right questions and helping their clients come up with their own solutions. Think of life coaching as a guiding light.

The client must do their own walking, climbing, digging, swimming, or whatever else to get to their desired destination.

While we provided a series of questions to ask your clients, as you gain experience, you will come up with many of your own. You will also become more aware of when and how to ask questions, which is equally important.

ARE YOU READY?

As a life coach, you will have the capability to change people's lives in ways you cannot imagine. An individual will look at life so differently after they have benefited from some good coaching session. While coaches are not miracle workers, they can help alter a person's reality, so a life they thought was once unattainable will now be something they actively work towards. The profession is difficult. There will be many challenges and a rollercoaster of emotions. However, the value it brings to clients is completely worth it. To watch someone who was once broken down rise up and face the world is an indescribable experience.

If you are ready to pursue this path, we urge you to take the information in this book and begin practicing it faithfully. We feel this book will serve as a great launching point for anyone who wants to become a life coach. At Elvin Coaches, we take our passion for being great coaches very seriously. Therefore, we are here to provide you support along your journey, as we want to build as many wonderful life coaches as possible.

We want to help as many people as possible with this information. If you found value in this book, please leave a review online so more people can become aware of it. Thank you again, and best of luck to you on your journey. We have faith in you!

Finally, if you did enjoy this book, we are about to make you much happier. This book is the first in what will be a series of similar topics. Our next book will be available soon in an advanced version to cover some of the sub-niche options in life coaching.

Just for you!

A FREE GIFT TO OUR READERS

Scan the QR code to subscribe or follow the link
https://elvinlifecoaches.activehosted.com/f/3

You're going to receive the

Wheel of Life Coaching Technique

and other goodies

REFERENCES

Adams, B. (2017, September 7). *6 Morning Rituals of Steve Jobs, Tony Robbins, Oprah, and Other Successful Leaders.* Inc.Com. https://www.inc.com/bryan-adams/6-celebrity-morning-rituals-to-help-you-kick-ass.html

Altmann, G. (n.d.). *Success Text.* Retrieved September 10, 2020, from https://www.pexels.com/photo/marketing-school-business-idea-21696/

Andrews, A. (n.d.). *Full Moon Illustration.* Retrieved September 9, 2020, from https://www.pexels.com/photo/full-moon-illustration-861443/

Arya, N. (n.d.). *Photography of Book Page.* Retrieved September 9, 2020, from https://www.pexels.com/photo/photography-of-book-page-1029141/

Autocratic. (n.d.). Coachingsportleadership.Weebly.Com. Retrieved September 4, 2020, from https://coachingsportleadership.weebly.com/autocratic.html#:~:text=The%20Autocratic%20coach%20takes%20on

Bertolazzi, I. (n.d.). *Neon Signage.* Retrieved September 10, 2020, from https://www.pexels.com/photo/neon-signage-2681319/

Blackbyrn, S. (2018, March 19). *Types of Coaching Styles And Models Every Coach Should Know About.* ..Coach; .Coach Blog. https://sai.coach/blog/types-of-coaching-styles/

Blackbyrn, S. (2019, December 30). *How To Become A Successful Mindset Coach: Convincing Clients Made Easy! - .Coach.* ..Coach; .Coach Blog. https://sai.coach/blog/how-to-become-a-successful-mindset-coach/

Bonham-Carter, D. (2007). *Life Coaching for Problem Habits - A Model for Life Coaches.* www.Davidbonham-Carter.Com. http://www.davidbonham-carter.com/article-modelofchange.html

Bundrant, M. (n.d.). *Top Five Obstacles To Becoming A Successful Business Coach And Their Solutions (Survey Results)» INLP Center.* INLP Center. Retrieved September 10, 2020, from https://inlpcenter.org/obstacles-for-business-coaches/

Casano, T. (2016, March 24). *11 Celebrities Who Prove Using A Life Coach Will Help Reboot Your Career*. Elite Daily. https://www.elitedaily.com/entertainment/celebrities-life-coach-career/1426180

Cesario, A. (n.d.). *Opened Glass Window*. Retrieved September 9, 2020, from https://www.pexels.com/photo/opened-glass-window-1906795/

Clear, J. (2018, July 13). *James Clear*. James Clear. https://jamesclear.com/new-habit

Colleen-Joy. (2018, May 18). *My top 20 Life Coaching Questions*. InnerLifeSkills. https://www.innerlifeskills.com/life-coaching-tools/my-top-20-coaching-questions/

Cook, C. (n.d.). *Photo of Blue Doorway*. Retrieved September 9, 2020, from https://www.pexels.com/photo/photo-of-blue-doorway-2929910/

C.S. Lewis Quote: Integrity is doing the right thing even when no one is watching. | Goalcast. (2018). Goalcast. https://www.goalcast.com/2018/03/26/15-c-s-lewis-quotes/c-s-lewis-quote1/

Davis, S. (n.d.). *Aircrafts Flying and Leaving Contrail*. Retrieved September 2, 2020, from https://www.pexels.com/photo/aircrafts-flying-and-leaving-contrail-4400026/

Elsey, E.-L. (2019, February 20). *10 of My All-Time Best Coaching Questions & Why! | The Launchpad - The*

Coaching Tools Company Blog. The Coaching Tools Company. https://www.thecoachingtoolscompany.com/10-time-best-coaching-questions/

Fauxels. (n.d.). *Man and Woman Near Table.* Retrieved September 9, 2020, from https://www.pexels.com/photo/man-and-woman-near-table-3184465/

Gavin de Becker Quotes (Author of The Gift of Fear). (n.d.). Www.Goodreads.Com. Retrieved September 5, 2020, from https://www.goodreads.com/author/quotes/31933.Gavin_de_Becker

Greater Minds. (n.d.-b). *What Is The Law Of Attraction? And How To Use It Effectively.* The Law Of Attraction. Retrieved September 1, 2020, from https://www.thelawofattraction.com/what-is-the-law-of-attraction/

Grushnikov, A. (n.d.). *Black and White Photos of Clocks.* Retrieved September 9, 2020, from https://www.pexels.com/photo/black-and-white-photo-of-clocks-707676/

Inner Glow Circle. (2019). What is Life Coaching and What Do Life Coaches Do?! (The Truth About Life Coaching) [YouTube Video]. In *YouTube.* https://www.youtube.com/watch?v=Ma1UWKLHrYQ&t=4s

Khan, S. (2019, July 13). *Six Benefits Of Working With A Business Coach.* Entrepreneur. https://www.entrepreneur.com/article/336762

Krasnow, P. (2018, April 18). *15 Habits for Earning Your Clients' Trust*. Outpost Blog. https://www.teamoutpost.com/blog/earning-clients-trust/

Ledwell, N. (n.d.). *HOW TO CHANGE YOUR BAD HABITS | Authentic Me | Nicky Massyn Life Coaching - Confidence, Well-being, Fertility Mindset - South West London*. Authentic Me. Retrieved September 9, 2020, from https://nickymassyn-lifecoach.com/blog/2019/3/15/how-to-change-your-bad-habits

Life Coach Insights: 3 Simple Strategies for Changing Habits. (2016, January 1). Jody Michael Associates. https://www.jodymichael.com/blog/3-simple-strategies-for-changing-habits/

Life Purpose Institute Admin. (2016, June 7). *7 Reasons To Become A Life Coach*. Life Purpose Institute. https://www.lifepurposeinstitute.com/7-reasons-to-become-a-life-coach/

Lonczak, H. (2020, April 16). *What's Your Coaching Approach? 10 Different Coaching Styles Explained*. Positive-Psychology.Com. https://positivepsychology.com/coaching-styles/#:~:text=It%20is%20a%20solution%2Dfocused

Lopes, H. (n.d.). *Four Person Standing on Cliff in Front of Sun*. Retrieved September 2, 2020, from https://www.pexels.com/photo/backlit-dawn-foggy-friendship-697243

Mentatdgt. (n.d.). *Two Woman Chatting*. Retrieved September 9, 2020, from https://www.pexels.com/photo/two-woman-chatting-1311518/

Miedaner, T. (2015). *What is a Life Coach? - LifeCoach.com*. LifeCoach.Com. https://www.lifecoach.com/what-is-a-life-coach/

Milanesi, M. (n.d.). *Photo of Mountain Under Starry Night Sky*. Retrieved September 9, 2020, from https://www.pexels.com/photo/photo-of-mountain-under-starry-night-sky-2670898/

Miller, B. (2020). *The 7 Common Challenges of Coaching*. Workboard.Com. https://www.workboard.com/blog/coaching-challenges.php

Mindvalley. (n.d.). *The Ultimate Guide of Powerful Coaching Techniques*. Evercoach. Retrieved September 6, 2020, from https://www.evercoach.com/ultimate-guide-of-powerful-coaching-techniques

Negative Space. (n.d.). *Person Writing on White paper*. Retrieved September 9, 2020, from https://www.pexels.com/photo/fashion-woman-notebook-pen-34072/

Pixabay. (n.d.). *Black Android Smartphone on Top of White Book*. Retrieved September 9, 2020, from https://www.pexels.com/photo/black-android-smartphone-on-top-of-white-book-39584/

Pixabay. (n.d.-b). *Clear Glass With Red Sand Grainer.* Retrieved September 9, 2020, from https://www.pexels.com/photo/clear-glass-with-red-sand-grainer-39396/

Pixabay. (n.d.-b). *Clear Light Bulb.* Retrieved September 9, 2020, from https://www.pexels.com/photo/abstract-blackboard-bulb-chalk-355948/

Pixabay. (n.d.-d). *Exit Signage Pointing at Right Side.* Retrieved September 9, 2020, from https://www.pexels.com/photo/arrow-communication-direction-display-235975/

Pixabay. (n.d.-d). *Human Fist.* Retrieved September 9, 2020, from https://www.pexels.com/photo/human-fist-163431/

Pixabay. (n.d.-f). *Pile of Rock Near Lake.* Retrieved September 9, 2020, from https://www.pexels.com/photo/balance-blur-boulder-close-up-355863/

Pixabay. (n.d.-g). *Question Mark illustration.* Retrieved September 9, 2020, from https://www.pexels.com/photo/ask-blackboard-chalk-board-chalkboard-356079/

Ratan Tata Quote: "None can destroy iron, but its own rust can! Likewise none can destroy a person, but its own mindset can!" (n.d.). Quotefancy.Com. Retrieved September 10, 2020, from https://quotefancy.com/quote/1439955/Ratan-Tata-None-can-destroy-iron-but-its-own-rust-can-Likewise-none-can-destroy-a-person

Roseplay, D. (n.d.). *Wooden Stamp on Ink Pad Placed on Desk*. Retrieved September 9, 2020, from https://www.pexels.com/photo/wooden-stamp-on-ink-pad-placed-on-desk-3839649/

Stewart, J. (2014). *Top Ten Myths About Life Coaching*. www.Schoolofcoachingmastery.Com. https://www.schoolofcoachingmastery.com/coaching-blog/top-ten-myths-about-life-coaching

The Coaching Academy Blog. (n.d.). *9 Key Ideas to Build and Change Your Habits | Blog | The Coaching Academy*. Www.the-Coaching-Academy.Com. Retrieved September 9, 2020, from https://www.the-coaching-academy.com/blog/9-key-ideas-to-build-and-change-your-habits-3185.asp

The Complete Guide to Intuitive Life Coaching. (n.d.). Life Coach Spotter. Retrieved September 6, 2020, from https://www.lifecoachspotter.com/intuitive-life-coach/#expectfrom

Tracy, B. (2018, August 17). *Business Coaching: A Guide to Everything You Need to Know | Brian...* Brian Tracy's Self Improvement & Professional Development Blog. https://www.briantracy.com/blog/business-success/business-coaching/

What is a Life Coach? Learn What Does a Life Coach Do To Help You. (2016). Tonyrobbins.Com. https://www.tonyrobbins.com/coaching/results-life-coach/

Wilson, G. (n.d.). *What are coaching styles and how do they work?* Www.Thesuccessfactory.Co.Uk. Retrieved September 7, 2020, from https://www.thesuccessfactory.co.uk/blog/coaching-styles-and-how-they-work

Winget, L. (2012, July 13). *Stop settling for average!* Larry Winget. https://www.larrywinget.com/stop-settling-for-average/

Weinschenk, S. (2019, April 19). *The Science of Habits.* Psychology Today. https://www.psychologytoday.com/gb/blog/brain-wise/201904/the-science-habits

WHO WANTS TO BE A SUPERHERO IF YOU CAN BE A BUSINESS COACH?

THE CORRECT AND SUCCESSFUL WAY TO BE A BUSINESS COACH

Just for you!

A FREE GIFT TO OUR READERS

Scan the QR code to subscribe or follow the link
https://elvinlifecoaches.activehosted.com/f/3

You're going to receive the

Wheel of Life Coaching Technique

and other goodies

INTRODUCTION

Imagine a young and ambitious adult who recently graduated from college. She received her degree in engineering and was hired by a major firm in her city. While the job paid well and her prospects were good, after a couple of years, she grew tired of being someone's employee. Most of all, she was getting tired of engineering. While in high school, she had dreams of starting a business, but the influential adults around her advised against it. It was too risky to start a business from scratch and they encouraged her to follow a safer path. As a result, she studied civil engineering in college and got a job in this field instead.

During college, she never developed a true passion for engineering even though she was amazing at math. After being with her employer for a couple of years, she was burned out and ready for something else. Unlike in high school, she was independent now and able to make more of her own decisions. Her goal now was to open a food truck and travel around town making unique meals. She was excited about this new change. However, she has no idea how to get started.

She does not want to ask any family members because they will only discourage her. She also does not know who else to turn to for solid advice. As a result, she is ready to give up on her dreams already. The stress, isolation, and fear of failure are not worth it.

In a situation like this, this young professional will benefit greatly from a business coach. Business coaching is a fascinating field where people get individual guidance in creating and developing their business ideas. A business coach has the ability to keep you on a directed path so that you make the best decisions in relation to your venture, whether they are financial, industry-related, marketing, or a wealth of other factors.

A business coach will never tell you what to do but will help you find the best answers within yourself. We all know ourselves best and sometimes it takes an objective viewpoint to understand which direction we must go. A business coach is a perfect individual for this.

Whether you are thinking about starting a business, are in the initiation phase, or have been running your business for a while, you will be struggling in many ways. There are many answers out there and it's difficult to determine what the ideal path is. The fear of starting a business and having it fail is very common. No matter how long a business has been running, the market is always changing, and the risk of losing everything always exists. A business coach can guide you in making sure this does not happen. They will help you come up with solutions based on your unique problems and also hold you accountable. The best part is, you will never feel like you are alone like so many business owners do.

As you go through the chapters of this book, you will gain a detailed understanding of what a business coach is and how they can help you as a business owner and entrepreneur. You will understand the many strategies and techniques that will guide you in becoming a successful business owner and not a statistic that is on the road to failure. In addition, we will discuss the many questions and information a business coach will have for you, so you can have an idea of how the process works. Asking the right questions at the right time and with the right demeanor is one of the foundations of good business coaching. Finally, we will go over some of the subspecialties within the business coaching umbrella.

Not only will you understand the process of working with a business coach, but whether or not you want to become one yourself. Since we are a part of the industry and recognize the many benefits it provides, we like to encourage other passionate people to join the field. Once you have read this book and realize how effective the practice is, there's a good chance you will want to join the coaching profession and assist others in the same manner. We are here to help you on your new journey.

Business

WHO ARE WE?

We are part of a collective known as Elvin Coaches. We have several members and decades of experience between all of us. We all met in Indonesia years ago and many of us were already practicing life coaches by then. This became a huge bonding moment between us and we have all grown as a family since then, supporting each other every step of the way.

We have all personally experienced the power that all forms of coaching has, both for the client and the coach. We learn from the people we help just as much as they learn from us.

All of us at Elvin Coaches are passionate about what we do that we wanted to get our knowledge and experience out to the masses. This is why we wrote this book as part of our series. We feel it is the best way for us to impart our knowledge to many people around the world. Whether you need the help of a business coach or want to become one yourself, we are here to help you. We want to make you a part of our family. Once you are, you will grow exponentially as a person through our step-by-step action plans we provide and be able to guide others to do the same.

(Fauxels, n.d.-b)

1

BUSINESS COACHING ON THE HIGHEST LEVEL

Business coaching is a subset of the broader art of life coaching. While life coaches generally assist clients in every area of their lives, business coaches are geared towards guiding clients in planning, initiating, and running a business. This includes helping them find answers to overcome real and potential threats to their business model.

Whether you are running a major corporation, a small business in your neighborhood, or work as an entrepreneur from home, there are specific challenges that come your way which you must be able to anticipate. These challenges might be common for all business owners, or unique to your industry or situation. The bottom line is, you will struggle immensely as a business owner through every process and the bigger your company becomes, the more potential problems there will be.

There is a lot of confusion out there about the difference between business coaching and consulting. The main separating factor is that a consultant will do the work for your business while the coach is more like a guiding presence who gives you the knowledge, training, tools, and guidance to do it yourself. For those wondering why it's more worthwhile to hire someone who will show you how to do it yourself versus someone who will do it themselves, the answer simply is that the business belongs to you.

As a business owner, in whatever capacity that might be, you must understand on your own what the best way to run and grow the business is. In the long run, it will be your responsibility and the issue with hiring a consultant is that once they are gone, all of the old problems related to past methods will return. When you hire a coach, you will do the work by finding the answers within yourself. Why is this better? Once again, it is your business and you are the one ultimately responsible for its success.

Think about the example of going to the gym and hiring a personal trainer. Why would you hire a trainer at the gym and pay them when you can just go in and start working out? Well, even if you use all of the equipment and go hard, you can still get zero to minimal results. You may not lose any weight or build any muscle. The trainer can help guide you by giving you exercises to target certain muscle groups and also provide instructions on meal planning. While the trainer will guide you,

you are responsible for doing the work. Unfortunately, we cannot become fit by other people exercising. At least, not just yet.

This idea holds true for hiring a business coach to help you with your business practices. You can just go in and start doing everything yourself, but that does not mean you will do it right. You could end up making massive mistakes that should have been avoided, but you were woefully unaware because you are not experienced in the business. Even if you are experienced, having an objective third party to give you instructions on maintaining the right path will still be helpful. Just like with a trainer, a business coach can help you with focus and targeted actions to minimize mistakes and bring in tremendous results, but they cannot and will not do the work for you.

The information, ideas, and skills you pick up from working with a business coach will last you a lifetime. So, even if the coach is gone, you can still succeed because you will have the answers within you. The following is a quick rundown of the many things a business coach can help you with:

- Setting better goals that are geared towards business growth.
- Coming up with action steps to reach said goals.
- Reaching goals at a faster rate.
- Making appropriate decisions that will lead to business growth.

- Improving relationships with customers, clients, partners, employees, and anyone else involved with the business.

Business coaching is not about what you have done in the past. That was an experience that you learned from. It is really about the future and the potential you can create for your organization. As coaching to over 100 clients over the years, we understand how valuable coaching can be to help owners achieve their goals.

As a business owner, you work for yourself and there is no one to motivate you except for yourself. There is no boss or predetermined deadlines. You do all of this yourself. Many individuals have a hard time finding the discipline or motivation to keep moving and stay on top of everything. Many people have no idea if they should do everything themselves or hire help. If they hire help, what kind of help will it be and how can they afford it on a shoestring budget? What programs exist to make business practices smoother? How can I reach my customer base? There are so many questions out there that business owners have and a business coach can help answer most, if not all of them.

Most of all, a business coach can hold you accountable. Most individuals work harder and do what they are supposed to do if they know someone is watching over them. Going back to the gym example, many patrons who go to workout simply do it lazily with little effort. On many occasions, they are spending more time on their phones and barely putting anything into their routines. Furthermore, they are only targeting specific areas on their bodies and completely ignoring others. A trainer can help gym-goers massively improve their workouts and outcomes, and business coaches can help you, as a business owner, do the same.

WHAT CAN A COACH REALLY DO?

To drive the point home about business coaches, we want to give you an in-depth perspective on what they can really do. As you have read this chapter so far, you are probably wondering why you can't just read a business book, attend a seminar, talk to a business owner, get a consultation, or speak to friends and family members. Why do you need to pay someone to tell you something you can learn for free? This last question can be debunked immediately because what a coach is able to tell you cannot be learned for free from anybody. If someone is actually helping you plan and personalize your path as a business owner to the extent a coach does and they are doing it for free, then they must really like you.

The truth is, all of the above options are beneficial to a degree. You can learn a lot from reading a book or talking to a business owner, but the personal guidance you will receive from any of these choices will be severely limited. For example, a business owner can give you advice, but maybe not personal advice specifically geared towards your business. A book or seminar will not be by your side to help you during unexpected moments. Friends and family might mean well, but they are often biased in their approach if they don't have the depth or breadth of knowledge necessary to properly advise.

A business coach will work as an objective third party who can give personal guidance at any point of business progression. They will be there to encourage you, but also hold your feet to the fire. When challenges arise, a coach will help you assess the situation and come up with the best answers for yourself. People who hire business coaches take a lot of solace in knowing they are not alone in their venture. Unfortunately, many business owners do feel this way, which is a shame. This is why it's important to recognize how useful business coaching can be.

So many startups fail before they even have a chance to get going. It's sad to think about the many amazing products or services that did not make it in this world because an individual did not know how to take it off the ground. They wanted to succeed but couldn't get past the barriers. It's time to start changing that. Business and entrepreneurship give you more potential for success than you could ever have dreamed possible. With all of the uncertainty of the world and job market, the ability to start a business has never been more attractive. The opportunities are endless as long as you know what you're doing. With a business coach, always knowing what to do next becomes much easier and less frightening.

One thing to understand is that coaches do not teach practical business skills. They will work more like a silent partner who is helping to hold you up. They will support your growth whether you are just starting, think about starting, or are highly experienced. Even successful business owners need coaches. You never know when bad decisions can cause a dramatic shift and a coach can help avoid things like this from happening.

Provide an Outside Perspective

The first thing a business coach can do is look at your situation as an outside observer with zero bias involved. From here, they can help you determine what is and isn't working for you and why. A good coach will help you recognize what your role is within the business and how it can align with your personal life in regards to your talents, core values, and vision.

An outside observer like a coach can also help determine where and when you are getting in your own way. Moments like these stunt the growth of your business and the more you can eliminate them, the better it will be for your progress.

Helps Establish Vision and Goals

Coaches help business owners set up the right individual vision and goals. It is crucial in any business to develop long-term goals that work well with what you're seeking in life. Having arbitrary symbols of success that don't relate to you in any way will not work in the long run. A coach helps align goals with people's values.

Coaches can uncover underlying inspiration for wanting success in business. Some examples include:

- Making a positve impact on the world.
- Having more autonomy to live a life that you want.
- Personal fulfillment and helping others solve a major problem.
- Creating jobs for people.
- Building wealth and leaving a legacy for your family.

Basically, a coach will help their clients figure out their "why" for starting a business. Whether a business is just a dream or a full-fledged organization, the "why" will always be important. If you don't know yours, then you are in danger of burning out and losing control.

A business coach will help you figure out your vision first and your goal second. This way, your business will follow what you truly value in life. If you are feeling directionless, getting help from an experienced coach can do wonders for you.

Goals!

Work With a Person's Strengths and Weaknesses

Everyone has their strengths and weaknesses, and that's okay. The problem occurs when people don't recognize where they are weak or if they don't take advantage of their strengths. A business coach can hold up a proverbial mirror so you can see these strengths and note the skills that you need to improve upon.

Building on strengths is a major shortcut to success. Being overly focused on what we're not good at, as many people are, can easily distract us from what we are already doing well. Coaches use a number of tools to determine how you learn, work, and relate to others. They will pick out areas where you shine and help you maximize these gifts to their full potential.

It's important to manage weaknesses, even if we can't turn them into strengths. The best thing to do here is to figure out how to not get tripped up by weaknesses to the point they halt your progress. Business coaches will help you discover the blind spots that are holding you back and then guide you towards growth, making your weaknesses ineffective.

Provide Accountability

Accountability is one of the most essential reasons for having a coach. It is easy to become lazy, not follow up on things, and take massive shortcuts. If we don't get caught, then what's the big deal? Well, if you're trying to run and build a business, then there's plenty that can go wrong. Not being held accountable can result in you going down the wrong direction. Business ownership is rewarding, but a long and arduous process every step of the way. During good and bad times, it is easy to lose sight of things and revert back to old habits or develop new bad habits. Luckily, a coach will help keep you on the right track and let you know when you're faltering.

Hiring a business coach is a sound investment that can significantly increase your potential and grow your business as you see fit. If you're still wondering how beneficial coaching can be, here are some questions to ask yourself:

- Do you want to work with someone who will challenge your thought process and make you think more deeply about yourself?
- Will it be helpful to have someone use intuitive tools and innovative practices to learn more about your business and what it needs? More importantly, what you need?
- Does the idea of maximizing your full potential get you excited?
- Are you willing to take responsibility for what you need to do?
- Remember that coaching is a collaborative practice where both parties involved do their part. The coach guides while the client listens and takes action.
- Are you ready to work and improve yourself by putting in the work every day?

If you answered yes to these questions, even just a few of them, then you are ready to enter the realm of business coaching. After working with a coach, you will have a new perspective on many facets of your business. You will finally be creating the type of life you deserve. If you like what you have read so far, you might be ready to become a business coach yourself.

WHY YOU'LL LOVE BEING A BUSINESS COACH

Life coaching is a great career to get into. Not only will you help people, but you will also learn more about yourself. Business coaching is one of the categories under the life coach umbrella. Business coaches can help those who are in some of their worst financial states to completely turn their lives around. Before discussing how to become a business coach, we will go over some of the advantages it provides.

You Double Your Rate of Personal Development

Becoming a coach and then practicing in the field will give you a two-for-one deal. As you become a coach, you will learn the strategies that help other businesses, and when you impart that knowledge on a client, you are learning again. Plus, you will learn about the diverse issues, some unique and unexpected, that your clients are going through. One of the best ways to learn something is to teach it.

As a coach, you are not required to be an expert on everything. In fact, there will be times you will know very little about the industry your client is involved in. That's okay because the techniques used in coaching will work across the spectrum. So, while you have to be well-versed in those techniques, you do not have to know everything about your client's business.

Make an Extraordinary Living

While money is not the main driving force behind coaching, once you become good at your craft, you will be highly sought out. This will lead to significant financial gain. Some great coaches out there are making a six-figure income in a year while some of the top coaches are making millions. While it may take a while to reach this point, if you keep honing your craft and getting better, there is no reason why you can't reach this level someday. You will be helping people at the highest level.

Building Lasting and Empowering Relationships

You will get to know your clients on an intimate level and will continue working with them for years. You will even be able to hold special events with them. You might even build up professional networks.

You Become an Expert in Business

As you work with clients to develop mastery in their business, you will develop mastery in your own. In the process, you will be practicing the techniques that you are teaching.

As business coaches help their clients explore ways to gain success, they are discovering their own methods at the same time. The truth is, if this is not occurring, you need to step up your game in regards to your coaching skills. Clients will believe in you more if you are practicing what you preach. It does not get any simpler than that.

You Become Well-Positioned for the Next Opportunity

As a coach, you receive front-row education about some of the top business ventures in the world. When you work with experienced business owners and help them navigate through tough waters, you pick up a lot of great information as well. You are getting paid to gain both business experience and education. Because of this education, you get to evaluate some of the best ideas out there. As a result, you will be poised to take on some of the greatest opportunities that come about in the future.

You Get to Give Your Gift

As a coach, you will learn some amazing techniques and strategies that can change a person's life. This is truly a gift and you get to give this gift every single day. Many coaches are in their coaching mindset even if they are not working with a client. The knowledge you receive gives you a different mindset of how you see the world and solve problems. Therefore, you will be benefiting people with your practices even if they are not your client.

Most people who go to work adopt a different personality. The ways they conduct themselves are completely different at home and in their place of business. As a coach, you can just be yourself all the time. Whenever you are interacting with someone in your life, they are receiving your coaching persona which becomes natural.

One issue this can raise is when you are just having a conversation versus actually providing free coaching. As a business coach, you have a valuable skill that helps business owners in a tremendous way. You must make sure you are being compensated properly and not being taken advantage of.

You Will be Appreciated

As you help people move from mediocrity to excellence with their businesses, you will gain a lot of appreciation from your clients. They will see you as part of their process in gaining wealth and will value the skills you bring.

HOW TO BECOME A BUSINESS COACH

If you believe it is too soon to become a business coach after just learning about the practice, don't be too quick to dismiss yourself. Just like any other business, developing a coaching practice requires specific actions, knowledge, and training. If you are reading this book, then you probably were thinking about starting a business anyway. If coaching interests you, then why not take this path.

Many individuals want to become a phenomenal business coach, but do not believe they have the qualifications, whatever those may be. What if we told you that there aren't any official qualifications, you just need to have specific goals, mindsets, and the desire to make a difference in the world. You don't have to necessarily go to a four-year university or pick up multiple types of certifications [though getting some certification is recommended]. Is it an easy road? Definitely not. However, once you go down the path, you will understand how rewarding the practice can be.

When you are developing a coaching practice, you have the opportunity to immediately put into practice what you are advising your clients. As you are helping your clients, you are learning how to help yourself too.

Business coaches change lives. They help people realize their dreams of being successful business owners. They inspire people to become the best versions of themselves. Finally, they develop strong and secure bonds with their clients. When you help that struggling business owner or aspiring entrepreneur become who they were meant to be, it gives you one of the biggest highs in the world. This alone is enough to inspire someone to get into the field. If you find all of this exciting, then coaching might be right up your alley.

What does it take to become a successful business coach? Just like any form of life coaching, it is an unregulated profession, so there is no formal training. This means anyone can become a business coach, which can certainly have its positives and negatives. Of course, the more credential and experience you have, the more credible your clients will find you. We will discuss building credibility more in chapter two.

It takes a lot of time, effort, and sacrifice to become a great coach. It does not happen overnight. Even when you reach a level of greatness, there is always more to learn. Your growth as a coach will never stop.

You may never become the perfect coach because nobody ever does. Improvements are essential to address and take care of. One of the best ways to ensure you will do well is to approach the field with a proper mindset, which we will discuss right here.

The Right Mindset

Becoming a business coach requires a certain mindset. This will be one of the main deciding factors on whether you have lifelong success or will fizzle out quickly. Your destiny as a coach will be decided by how your mind works. If you have a poor mindset, then you will create poor results. The good news is, your mindset is something you can control. The problem is, many coaches, old and new, don't realize that their way of thinking could be causing them to fail. This is why we wanted to address this with you right away.

Having multiple years of coaching between all of us, Elvin Coaches believe in having a specific attitude when approaching the field of business coaching. The following are some of the traits you must develop if you are to enter the field of coaching and become successful.

Self-Belief

The bottom line is, if you do not believe in yourself, then no one else will believe in you either. Successful business coaches have 100% belief in their skills, products, and services and they are not afraid to share them. They know for a fact they can help others and in your quest to become a coach, you must feel the exact same way.

Lifelong Learner

Successful coaches ever stop learning because they know they are far from perfect, no matter how good they become. They are always looking for ways to improve their personal and professional growth and are willing to invest in their education. The best coaches are always on the lookout for courses, seminars, engagements, and even opportunities to get mentored. No matter how much you learn as a coach, never believe that you know it all.

Purposeful

They have a strong purpose behind what they do that goes well beyond making money. While you can certainly create a great income as a coach, just ask Tony Robbins or Brian Tracy, this should not be your ultimate purpose for becoming one. There needs to be a bigger "why" behind all of this. This can be helping someone realize their dreams or changing people's lives.

Accountable

Business coaches follow their own lead of holding others accountable by also holding themselves accountable. You must do this in order to get the results you desire and become focused on your goals and dreams.

Driven

Business coaches are driven to become the very best they can be at all times. They have a high level of ambition and are motivated to keep going. They are not afraid of hard work and doing what it takes to make it to the top.

Brave

All great coaches are brave enough to tell their clients what they need to hear and not what they want to hear. This is the essence of coaching because clients who are constantly praised for everything only get a bloated ego and don't have any real growth. Business coaches are not seeking praise. They genuinely want to help their clients and this can mean making them feel uncomfortable at times.

Service-Oriented

Business coaches are in the field of service. They enjoy helping as many people as they can and contributing in some way to their success. We can tell you from experience that watching someone turn their lives around because of the help you gave them as a coach produces a tremendous high.

Overall, business coaches need to be motivating, dedicated, helpful in setting up performance plans, and be very empowering. As a business owner as well as a coach, you will need to know when to delegate and manage your time appropriately. Items you can delegate can be things like marketing, website development, sending emails, or making phone calls, etc. Chapter three of this book will get heavy into time management.

As you can see, these mindset tactics are not exclusive to coaching. they can be utilized for success in any area of your life. To reach the highest level in any field, you must be fully committed.

Specializing

Once you have decided that to become a coach and understand the mindset that is involved, another factor to consider is the type of business coach you want to become. Business coaching is a subset of life coaching and from here there are many more categories to consider. You can certainly be a general business coach and help every type of business owner to a certain degree. On the other hand, you can become specialized and work with a niche group of people. This second option may give you the potential for more income, but a lot of that will have to do with marketing and how you present yourself.

Some examples of specializing include:

- Helping a specific age group like Millennials or Gen-Z, who are new to the business world.
- Working with single moms who want to become entrepreneurs.
- Working with online business owners.
- Coaching those who want to get into sales and marketing.

Working with a specific niche is a great way to get extra attention. You can start speaking to a specific group of people.

A Few More Steps

We will end this chapter by going over a few general steps on how you can get your coaching practice up and running. Remember, coaching is a passion, but you must also treat it like a business. That is the only way you will continue to get clients and keep your practice afloat. Here is a quick and easy guide to start your practice and build it to the next level:

Join a Network

A network is a group of people who are on a similar mission as you. In order to get your coaching business known, you can set up your own marketing campaigns, but you can also join various networking groups, including specific coach or business groups. Joining a group like this will introduce you to like-minded people and you guys can share your passion and promote each other's work in the community. You will also gain a lot of education by doing this.

Create a Business Plan

Starting a business without a plan is like building a house without a blueprint. You should never do it. A solid business plan will help you determine exactly what you need to do, how you will do it, how you will fund it, and how quickly you will get it done. The plan is not just for starting the business, but also running and growing it in the future. A business plan will give you complete clarity in how you will proceed with your coaching business. FYI, as a business coach, you may find yourself assisting many of your clients in creating their own business plan.

Make Sure You Have Capital

The good news is, coaching does not require a lot of capital compared to many other business ventures. However, you will still need some finances for marketing purposes and to live off of while you are developing your practice.

Secure Your Own Coach

While you are working on becoming a coach, secure your own business coach who can guide you along the way. Imagine the massive learning opportunities both of you will have.

Have a Solid Marketing Plan

If you start up a coaching practice but have no clue how you will get leads or find new clients, you are setting yourself up for failure. It does not matter how good of a coach you are, if people do not know you exist, then you will not be successful. Having a solid marketing plan is essential in this regard. Your marketing plan needs to clearly state what you do and who your target group, or niche, is, and how you are going to reach out to them. Marketing is one of the toughest and most important aspects of the business. It is how you get your clients.

Be Consistent

As a coach, you must remain consistent with what you do. For example, with marketing, you cannot jump around from one thing to another. You must focus on a few things to see if they work for you, or not. Once you have given the strategies an opportunity, then you can move on if needed. However, you must be consistent for long term success.

Always Improve

As a coach, you must always find ways to improve yourself. You must also keep up with new techniques and strategies that are beneficial for your clients and your practice. This is why it's important to read, attend seminars and workshops, and join networking groups.

Now that you understand what a business coach does and how to create a successful practice, we will get into more specific topics related to the field. By the end of the book, you will gain an in-depth idea of exactly what a business coach can do and how to be successful as one yourself.

(Juhaszimrus, n.d.)

2

THE ESSENCE OF BUSINESS COACHING CREDIBILITY

Trust

In any type of business you decide to get into, you need to find people to buy your product and/or service. This can take a lot of effort as there are so many moving parts. One of the things potential clients look for is credibility. Once again, this is not something that is built up overnight. The same holds true for business coaching. As a coach, you need to build up your credibility so that your clients will trust you enough to give you a chance. Remember, many of them will be in vulnerable states and they might be very cautious about who they can trust. When you have some credibility behind your name, the chances of clients seeking out your services will increase greatly. If you do a great job, your reputation will grow.

Unfortunately, many business owners forget about this aspect and end up jumping into the deep end of the pool right away. They begin creating outlandish coaching programs, running expensive marketing campaigns, and charging ridiculous prices for their services. These coaches are not in the profession to help people, they are here just to make money, and that's the wrong approach to take. Making money is an extra benefit that comes from being an excellent coach, but it should never be the main reason to go into the profession. It should not be your "why." If it is, your clients will see right through it and you will not have any credibility at all.

From the moment you start coaching on your first day, your focus needs to be on creating results for your client. They are coming to you because they need help with their business and your job is to be there for them to the best of your ability. Yes, marketing and putting yourself out there is important. However, when you help your business clients gain results, it will speak volumes for you. Your reputation will spread like wildfire through the mouths of the people you work with, so do your best to make sure they are speaking well of you.

HOW TO BUILD CREDIBILITY

As a business coach, you will be a mentor to your clients, and it is important to be credible in this regard to gain optimal success in the field. Your reputation, and therefore, your credibility, rests heavily on your clients trusting you. Even if you're acting like your authentic self with your clients, establishing credibility will be much more difficult than you think. Remember that your clients do not know you on a personal level. They may not know whether or not you're being honest with them. That's why it's important to do whatever you can to build up some trust.

Establishing trust early on will set the tone for the relationship you have with your clients and will give you something to build off of for the remainder of the time you are together. The question now is, how do we build trust and credibility with our clients? The focus of this chapter will be to discuss the most effective techniques for building a strong rapport with your coaching clients. Once you create this type of relationship, you will develop credibility in their eyes.

Build a Foundation

Create some social media accounts related to your coaching practice and, at least a couple of times a week, put out helpful content that potential clients will see and gain value from. These posts should be written for the sole purpose of engaging people and providing them helpful information. It should not have a sales tone to it. Your goal is to build a foundation with these posts so that people can see that you know what you're talking about. After reading these posts, business owners will be able to know exactly how you can help them. Think about your social media as a window into who you are. Every time you write anything on there, you are showing a part of yourself.

Stay on the Path

Establishing a voice and your brand is one of the hardest things to do in business. Having a consistent voice that views problems and solutions through a single lens can help establish a coach and client relationship. Your voice should express who you are because it will attract the clients that are meant to work with you. You will not be the right coach for everybody and that's okay. When you are working with the clients who will benefit from you, you will make a successful coach.

Gather Credentials

We already established that coaching is a largely unregulated profession, but that does not mean your clients will not be looking for credentials. Whether you like it or not, people are attracted to degrees and certifications that show some type of training. We are not asking you to get a college degree. However, getting some credentials is definitely a good idea. When you are a new coach, you will not have the benefit of reviews and people speaking highly of you. Getting some certifications can make you look more professional.

The International Coaching Federation or ICF is a good organization to go through. Furthermore, just because the coaching profession is not highly regulated now, it does not mean it won't be in the future. Some organizations are already asking for coaches to have certification. You might as well be ahead of the curve.

Teach From Experience

There are many experts, but not enough practitioners. People are more interested in your actions than they are your words. If you talk the talk but cannot walk the walk, then you will lose rapport with your clients in the end. If you want to establish credibility in the market, make sure you are living the way you teach others. If you are guiding your client and they can see that your actions match your words, they will view you as a credible coach who believes in what they are saying. Be a practitioner of your own teachings.

Be Real

Your clients are not looking for a fake persona. They are looking for you to be your unique self. When your clients start to see you as a real person who is also learning and living, they will start to trust and relate with you much more. Don't be afraid to speak from the heart and show them the real you. Don't divulge details of your life that neither you nor your client would be comfortable with. That's unprofessional. Just loosen up and give them a small taste of who you are.

Be Remarkably Different

People are not going to be attracted to you because you are a cookie-cutter version of everyone else. Being remarkably different and your own person will give you more credibility with your clients. To do this, you must determine your values, voice, and personal views. After this, create a unique value proposition for your clients. Clients want to be treated as individuals, and if you are showing that you're different from everyone else, it will assert some credibility for you in this regard. People will be more comfortable around you if they can see you are not just a carbon copy of other coaches.

Rave About Your Case Studies

As you serve more clients and help them benefit, your credibility will soar. Don't be afraid to let the public know how you helped people in the past. If some of your clients are willing to give you positive reviews, that's a good thing, as well.

Offer Value All the Time

Every time you are coaching a client, whether in person, over the phone, a video conference call, or simply emailing them some information, you must offer them value at all times. You must always strive to be at your best because it will build your credibility and it is not fair to your client if you don't.

In addition, you must offer value through various channels like social media, YouTube videos, or group chats. These are your opportunities to market yourself for free and show the public that you have a lot to offer. You don't have to put on full coaching sessions for free, but give your potential clients a taste of what you're about.

Solve Client Problems

The easiest and most effective way for a business coach to gain credibility is to help solve their client's problems as masterfully as possible. A client seeks out a business coach because they want strong guidance in creating a solid business. They want to overcome problems swiftly as they come upon them. This is what they want, so this is what you must give them. When you do, then they will know you are legitimate. When their friends and associates ask them how they were able to build up their business so well, they will tell them about you. Instantly, you just got a word-of-mouth shoutout. The more solutions you provide, the more credibility you will naturally gain.

Get Visible Immediately

If you want to make a name for yourself, whether it's with coaching or anything else, you must make yourself visible. You cannot hide in a bunker and expect people to know about you. Get out there on social media, YouTube, podcasts, and any other platform you can to get people to know about you. Nowadays, anyone can create podcasts or YouTube channels, so there's an extra benefit there. If you are willing to do speaking engagements, get out there and speak where you can. Be as visible as you can.

Be Trustworthy, Consistent, and Genuine

These three attributes are the cornerstone of credibility. People must know you are there to help them and not just in it for the money. Focus on improving these three principles and you will slowly build your credibility.

Be An Active Student and Contributor

Actively engage in the art of coaching with all of your heart and mind. Seek out professional training, read books, go to seminars, get a coaching mentor yourself, and do whatever you need to keep on learning. The more you are willing to improve your craft, the more credible you will become in the industry.

Hitch Your Wagon to Someone Else's Star

There are many coaching practices already out there with credibility and a strong reputation. Become a subcontractor with them and you will soon learn firsthand how to run a successful coaching business, the client and coaching process, marketing tips, and get a lot of firsthand experience. By being attached to an established brand, you will gain a lot of exposure in every aspect.

Many of the top coaches in the world have their own certification programs like John Maxwell or Tony Robbin. Getting certification through one of their programs can be greatly beneficial for you too.

Always Be Understanding

People have a desire to be understood. One of the major steps in gaining credibility is to demonstrate sincerity in understanding where your clients are at in their lives, their feelings, and what they are currently experiencing. After this, you must show your client that you can guide them to a proper solution that they may not be able to reach on their own. You are not telling them what to do, you are helping them find their own answers.

Volunteer in Visible Ways

Volunteering in your industry can be a great way to gain experience, connections, and credibility. Examples of places for volunteering in this manner include nonprofit organizations, colleges, and universities, or mission-driven organizations.

WHAT TO AVOID AS A COACH

Not only do you need to know how to gain credibility as a coach, but you must also know what to avoid doing. Mistakes can cost you a lot and put a complete halt to your coaching practice before it even has a chance to get off the ground. The following are some fatal errors you want to avoid at any point during your coaching process.

· · ·

Fixing

Many people who like to help others become accustomed to stepping in and doing everything themselves. As a coach, this is something you want to avoid. Remember the example of the personal trainer from chapter one. Just like a trainer, a coach cannot fix their client's problems. they can simply guide them into finding their own answers. If you end up correcting all of your client's problems on your own, they will not know what to do when you're not around. Eventually, they will fall apart and will blame you for your poor coaching skills. Plus, you don't want to get the reputation of someone who simply fixes people's problems. Clients will just start taking advantage of you if this occurs.

Interrupting

As a coach, you are there to listen to your client and provide guidance. You are not there to interrupt and interject with your own points of view. Ask followup questions as appropriate, ask for clarification when needed, but don't interrupt. Wait until your client is done or a pause before you start speaking. Your client deserves to let all of their feelings out and will become frustrated if you constantly put up blockades that prevent them from speaking.

Distracted Coaching

Whether you are coaching online or in-person, avoid distracted coaching at all costs. This means limiting environmental noise.

Go to a peaceful cafe for a meeting rather than a loud restaurant. If possible, choose some type of office setting. When you are coaching, remain fully engaged. Don't try to multitask by doing other activities while trying to coach. Even if you are skilled at multitasking, you will either not be able to give your client the attention they deserve or won't appear to be giving that attention during a session and that is not fair to them.

Stacking Questions

The concept of stacking questions means that you are asking your client more than one question at a time. On the outset, this can cause mass confusion and make your client feel overwhelmed. Ask one question at a time and allow the client to answer fully before asking another question.

Checklist Coaching

Checklist coaching means that you are using a predetermined list of questions rather than targeted ones geared towards your client's needs. Remember that you want to look unique as a coach and checklist coaching means you are just following some status quo approach. Also, your client will have their personal set of issues they need to deal with, so using a cookie-cutter approach like checklist coaching will just make them feel like they are part of a crowd and not an individual person.

Being Diagnostic

This goes along the lines of telling your clients what to do. When you are being diagnosed, you are asking your client-specific questions and making targeted suggestions, like, "Have you tried this?" or "This is what you should do." This is the wrong path to take when coaching and more so falls within the lines of consulting. As a coach, you need to ask more open-ended questions without giving your clients definitive answers.

Getting Trained on the Client's Time

With each client, you will learn and improve your skills. That's a given. However, you cannot start taking clients until you can offer them something valuable. Therefore, before you start coaching on your own, get practice in other ways, like training with a partner, sitting in on coaching sessions, going through a qualified training program, or a combination of all of these. Do not get trained on the client's time.

Failing to Put in Ways to Track Progress

Coaching is about getting results for your client. You must also have a way to track these results so both parties can see the progress that's been made. Find your own unique ways to measure changes that have occurred.

Leading on a Client You Cannot Help

At some point, you may need to cut the cord with a client. You will not be the right coach for everybody. Once you realize that you don't have a connection for whatever reason, be honest with your client about it and refer them to a new coach. Do not lead them on if you don't think you can help them. A client will appreciate your honesty more than fake help.

All of these habits will put a bad taste in your client's mouth about you and the coaching profession, in general. You must avoid these habits at all costs. Once your reputation starts to suffer, it will be difficult to rebuild.

I hope you enjoyed these tips to help you increase your credibility as a business coach. The reputation of an entrepreneur means a lot for their success. Credibility leads to a positive reputation. Always remember that with anything you do with your coaching practice.

WHY VULNERABILITY IS IMPORTANT

Vulnerability

A common misconception throughout history is that the strongest people among us never show emotion, are always closed off, and avoid anything that makes them appear vulnerable. The truth is, vulnerability is extremely important for progress to be made. In the field of business coaching, we rely on our clients to become vulnerable insofar as they can communicate the extent of their problems, and as such help them the most. If a client remains closed off, there is no chance of reaching them. Since a vulnerable person does put their guard down and open themselves up emotionally, it is a true sign of strength. Here are some major reasons why vulnerability is so important and why you should start embracing it.

Vulnerability Allows Advancement

Making yourself vulnerable is a scary prospect. Trying anything new for the first time can be quite nerve-racking. It's okay to feel fear, but it's not okay to let this fear stop you from moving forward. You need to expand your comfort zone by taking some chances. When you take chances, you are making yourself vulnerable because you are entering unfamiliar territory where you don't know what is going to happen. In terms of a coaching session, this means opening up emotionally, allowing you to advance.

Vulnerability Leads to Increased Abilities

When you are guarding yourself, it means you are fearful of something, like getting harmed physically or emotionally, getting exposed, or a number of other things that threaten your safety. However, if you are willing to be vulnerable in a safe setting, you are getting past your fear of the unknown. A major fear that people have is that of failing. They hate the thought of failing at something and are worried about looking foolish. They have negative voices in their head telling them they can't do something. When they give in to these voices, they are refusing to be vulnerable.

Once you learn how to be vulnerable, you start taking risks. Remember that anytime you step out of your comfort zone, you are making yourself vulnerable. Even walking out of your home has an element of vulnerability to it. Once you start embracing this idea, you will accomplish more goals, challenge yourself more often, and increase your abilities, in general.

A client who becomes vulnerable is more likely to set out on specified action plans. This will lead to more desired results.

Vulnerability Allows Openness With Others

Once someone accepts their vulnerability, they become much more open about their lives. They will usually not hesitate to express any of their emotions. This can be a double-edged sword, depending on who a person's friends are. If they are close to other people who appreciate openness, it can be a good thing.

Having an openness to share is a huge blessing for any business coach. The more vulnerable a client is, the less exploration a coach will have to do in order to find answers. The more trust you establish with a client ahead of time, the more vulnerable they are willing to be.

Vulnerable Allows Openness to Self

Not only will vulnerability allow you to be more open with the public, but also more open and honest with yourself. Being vulnerable increases self-confidence because you are more willing to put yourself on the world's stage. You are inviting people to get to know you, both negative and positive aspects. By doing this, you are also opening yourself up for criticism which is truly brave. The more criticism you are willing to receive, the stronger you will grow.

As a coach, having a client who is open with themselves will also be more courageous in sharing during coaching sessions. They will also go out after a session and take chances which means they will follow through on their plans without becoming fearful.

Vulnerability Makes it Comfortable to be in Discomfort

Being vulnerable is all about leaving your comfort zone and becoming uncomfortable. As with anything else, the more often you put yourself in uncomfortable settings, the more you will get used to them. As a result, you will become more comfortable and willing to put yourself in vulnerable situations. The more you expose yourself to vulnerability, the greater potential for success you will have.

Other benefits of vulnerability include:

- Having more self-acceptance. Not being afraid of who you are, flaws, and all.
- Engaging in more real and truthful conversations.
- Attracting the right kind of people in your life.
- Being empathetic will be much easier.
- Strengthening the bond of many of your relationships.
- Appearing more humanized in other people's eyes. Most people don't like being around those who appear perfect all the time. They appreciate those who are willing to show some of their flaws.

Here's the bottom line, being vulnerable is scary, but it makes life more exciting and worth living. That old adage of nothing gets done inside of a comfort zone holds a lot of truth. To accomplish your goals and live the life you desire, you have to take chances which means you have to become vulnerable. As a coach, this is something you must also get across to your clients. Being a coach, it is important to have clients who are willing to be vulnerable, otherwise, you will get nowhere. In addition, if someone is planning to start a business, they will need to put themselves in positions of vulnerability often.

HELP YOUR CLIENT BECOME VULNERABLE

Since there are so many advantages to being vulnerable and being in this state will vastly improve the relationship between a coach and client, it is in your best interest as a coach to help your clients become more vulnerable. Ultimately, it is up to them how open they want to be, but here are a few ways you can guide them.

Help Them Accept That They Are Worthy

Before a person can become vulnerable, they must recognize that they are worthy of receiving a positive response from the world. Help them believe that who they are is enough to warrant love. Basically, a person needs to know and believe they are capable of reaching their goals.

As a coach, you can help your clients in this regard by reinforcing the fact that they are worthy. This is where asking great follow up questions comes in. When a client is able to reach their conclusion with the help of your guidance, they will start believing they can achieve what they want in life.

> *"...The people who have a strong sense of love and belonging believe they are worthy of love and belonging. That's it. They believe they are worthy."*
>
> — BRENE BROWN, VULNERABILITY RESEARCHER

Understand What a Person's Skittish Tendencies Are

Many people who are on the cusp of showing vulnerability will have a knee-jerk reaction at the last minute and retreat back to their familiar environment. That environment is one of being guarded. This reaction will seem appropriate in the moment, but most people will regret it once they feel they are in a safe place. Making the final jump when you are at that moment of truth is a better option that will make you happier in the end.

As a coach, there will be many moments where certain clients will be right there on the edge. They will want to open up but are not quite there yet. It will be very easy for them to retreat and without your intervention, they are more likely to do that. If you notice this hesitation or skittishness, you can guide and encourage your clients to keep moving towards vulnerability by using the skills of listening and asking appropriate questions. We will go over these skills later in this book.

One technique you can use with your client is to write down the emotions they feel when they are hesitant to be vulnerable. These emotions can be triggers and being aware of them can help in avoiding them in the future.

Help Clients understand They Can Deal With an Outcome

It is a horrible feeling when you put your emotions out there and get nothing back. However, once this happens, you feel the hurt, but that's as far as it goes. After feeling the pain and pulling yourself back up, you know that you can handle the aftermath of being vulnerable.

Help your clients understand this too. Have them discuss past moments of pain by putting themselves out there. Remind them that they are still here which means they survived. As a coach, you must also be a listening ear as they share their vulnerability. never dismiss or downplay their emotions because they are real to them.

Share Hurt With Others

Once again, you are in the perfect position as a coach to let your clients share their feelings and emotions. As your clients open up about their pain, whatever it may be, you have the opportunity to be a non-judgmental ear. As you are listening to your client, give them the time they need to fully express themselves before asking more questions. Never make them feel like they're being rushed. The more practice they get at being vulnerable, the better they will be at it.

Help Your Clients Realize They are on the Way Up

Avoiding vulnerability is actually counterproductive. People feel that they are protecting themselves when they remain closed off. However, they are just harming themselves more through inaction. Think about all of the benefits that come from vulnerability and now imagine that you are depriving yourself of all of them. This will continue to keep you in a state of disappointment.

Vulnerability does also have the potential to cause harm. That's always the case when you are taking a risk. However, if you try and fail, at least you will know. You can move on. If you remain closed off, you will stay at the bottom and never grow. If you are already at the bottom, the only way to go is up. As a coach, you can help your clients realize this through thoughtful questioning.

We spoke about credibility earlier. Credibility leads to trust, and trust leads to comfort. When your clients are comfortable around you, they are more likely to become vulnerable. Always work on building your credibility as a business coach.

THE IMPORTANCE OF PRIVACY

All of us at Elvin Coaches have worked with countless clients who have expressed their deepest concerns, desires, goals, fears, and feelings. Oftentimes, our clients will tell us things that their best friends and closest family members do not know. They put a lot of trust in us by doing this and we must all remember to take this trust very seriously.

This is why it is important to always maintain privacy when working with a client. Treat the information they give you like you would handle protected medical information. It is not appropriate to discuss what your clients tell you with other people. What happens in the session should stay in the session.

3

TIME MANAGEMENT TIPS TO INCREASE PRODUCTIVITY

"The key is not in spending time, but investing it."

— STEPHEN R. COVEY

Time management is such a critical subject that many books already cover. Time management is a skill that is highly necessary but woefully ignored by many segments of the population. This is a shame because so many goals and dreams get crushed because people do not use this essential resource well. As the above quote suggests, our time must be invested because it is the most valuable resource we have.

A subset of business coaching is time management coaching. Many coaches and managers alike, will immediately review a client or employee's general performance and immediately come to the conclusion that their time management skills are poor. Furthermore, as they view their existing options for increasing performance, they feel that none of them will be beneficial. The truth is, in order to make a lasting difference, coaches need to look outside the box beyond the limited options in front of them to create a much larger context for their clients to succeed.

(Chuangch, n.d.)

TIME MANAGEMENT COACH STRATEGIES

As we mentioned earlier, you can make time management a major part of your program as a business coach or become a time management coach exclusively. In this section, we will go over some options you have as a time management coach to help your clients in this regard.

Give Them a Bunch of Tips

With this approach, it is as simple as observing someone as they function through the day and randomly tossing them tips on how to manage their time. For example, you can randomly say, "A planner is a great way to keep your schedule organized," or "Have you tried a to-do list before?" This strategy is not the best because time management is based on the accumulation of a number of habits that are developed over time. You can't break these habits simply by telling someone to do something. Just like it takes a while to build, it will take a while to break and reform.

Changing habits means you must shift many ingrained patterns of behavior. Some people have held onto their habits since they were small children and learned from the influential adults in their lives. Before you attempt your first coaching session, it helps to know and understand what specific habits your client has. From here, you can systematically help them shift from their good to bad habits for improving time management.

Buy a Book

Buying someone a book can be a better option than tossing tips because it gives a client something concrete to look at to obtain some time management advice. The only problem here is that everyone gets their own interpretation from reading a book. This is not necessarily a bad thing, but coaches must realize their clients will not do things just as they do.

Also, from a book, you get a singular approach to handling a situation. We are all different from each other and that means a one-size-fits-all method may not be very effective. A customized approach is much more useful for coaching clients, and in reality, that is your job as a business coach. A book is an okay option, but you should also review it with them and see what they think. Therefore, make sure it is a book you have read and understand well.

Time Management Program

This can be a good option too and a client may get more personalized attention, but still not to the extent of working with a coach. Another major issue with time management programs is the lack of followup. Participants will leave feeling inspired but revert back to their old habits because they have taken no real action to make habit changes.

Effective Techniques for Time Management

The following are some general steps for creating good time management that you can help your clients achieve.

Scheduling

Creating a tangible schedule is essential for making sure you get everything you need to be done completed. You can use a scheduling app on your phone or a physical planner, whichever one you prefer. When making a schedule:

- Create a long-term plan, preferably about a month, or several months in advance.
- Assess that work that needs to be completed weekly and daily.
- Adjust the plan based on specific needs.

Create a Daily Checklist

- Spend five to ten minutes each day planning your activities using a to-do list.
- Review and prioritize your list before you get moving. Make sure you are doing the most important and complicated tasks first.
- Break down the complicated tasks into smaller and manageable steps.
- As you complete items, check them off your list. It's important to finish one task before moving onto the next one.

Create a Habit

- Establish a routine of completing these lists.
- Spend time each week reviewing your list and goals. This is to make sure you are keeping up and assessing for any changes in your plan.
- Reward yourself when sticking to your routines.
- Keep a calendar of your long-term schedule with you.

Balance Your Life

- Make every minute of your day count.
- Prioritize your tasks from the most important to least important.
- When you are focused on a task or activity, remain committed to it without distractions. When you are working, focus on working. When you are spending time with friends, remain fully engaged with them.
- Don't procrastinate.

Time

WHY PROCRASTINATION IS BAD

We certainly cannot talk about time management without discussing it's close relative, procrastination. Procrastination is a major productivity killer and probably the greatest culprit in creating poor time management. Procrastination basically means you are putting off something for later that can be done now. In most cases, this is an important task that has a deadline but is not very appealing to work on. As a result, people will substitute something less important or a time-wasting for the task they don't want to work on. As a result, they get closer to the deadline and will have less time to get it done. This will lead to more stress and anxiety which will also cause a reduction in performance.

When you procrastinate, you are not using your time well. Imagine having a project that is due at the end of the week. You can start it on Monday and put in a couple of hours each day so that on the final day, you will just have to touch a few things up. Instead, you don't work on it on Monday, Tuesday, or Wednesday, and then on Thursday, you realize the mistake you made. Not only do you have to work on the project from scratch, but you also have to make sure it is presentable. Procrastination can affect us in many ways and it is a habit we need to get rid of.

Procrastination is often confused with pure laziness. This is not the case. There are usually some more underlying issues going on like having a fear of failure, fear of success, being a perfectionist, or having some underlying emotional issues. Furthermore, extended procrastination can lead to more mood disorders down the line. The following are some steps you can help your clients with if they display signs of being a procrastinator.

Recognize Being a Procrastinator

If a person is delaying important tasks for a genuinely good reason, like something more urgent coming up or taking some time to think about a project before jumping in, then it's not actually procrastination. It is a purposeful delay. However, if they are putting things off indefinitely or for no apparent reason, then procrastination is the culprit. Some other signs of procrastination include:

- Filling up the day with low-priority tasks.
- Leaving items on a to-do list for long periods of time.
- Getting distracted constantly while working on something important.
- Doing unimportant tasks for other people.
- Not knowing how to say no.
- Waiting to be in the right mood to complete a task.

The first step in solving a problem is acknowledging that you have one. As a time management coach, help your client figure out if they are procrastinators.

. . .

Work Out the Reason for Procrastination

After figuring out someone is a procrastinator, the reasons behind the habit must be determined. As we stated earlier, it is generally not related to laziness and there are usually more underlying reasons. For example, are you procrastinating on something because you find it boring and tedious? The best thing to do in this situation is to get it out of the way as quickly as possible. This way, you can stop worrying about it and move on. Why keep something in the back of your mind that you don't want there?

Poor organization, fear, overconfidence, and perfectionism are all common reasons for procrastination. Work with your client to determine why they are procrastinators.

Adopt Some Anti-Procrastination Strategies

Procrastination is a deeply ingrained habit and if your client is like most people, many of those around them were probably the same way. Habits only stop controlling us when we actively stop doing them. Below are a few strategies to tell your client so they can kick the self-defeating habit of procrastination:

- Forgive yourself for procrastinating in the past. There is nothing you can do about past mistakes, so it's best to let them go and move on. This will give you a more positive view of yourself.
- Commit to a task and focus on doing instead of

avoiding. Specify a time for completing your tasks. A trick you can use is to make a personal deadline that is a couple of days earlier than the actual deadline.
- Promise yourself a reward if you complete a difficult task on time and an even bigger reward if you complete it a little early.
- Have someone hold you accountable. When we feel someone is watching us, we tend to be more careful with what we do.
- Take care of things as you go. People have a tendency to ignore items as they become aware of them. However, it is better to tackle them from the get-go as long as it's not interrupting an important task. For example, if you get some important emails, answer them right away. If an appliance breaks, take care of it ASAP. If you need to make some phone calls, get them over with. As you put off the small things, they will slowly build up into a large pile.
- Minimize distractions by turning off your social media, avoid answering emails, work in a quiet area, let people know not to bother you during certain hours, and don't keep anything on your desk that does not need to be there.

Many of the time management techniques we will address later will also help you with procrastination. Get rid of this evil cousin of time management and you will be surprised at the progress you make. Of course, procrastination is not the sole reason for poor time management, so you may need to dig a little deeper to figure out.

HOW TO BUILD A HABIT

Proper time management has a lot to do with the habits you develop. Habits are the tendencies you develop over time and directly affect what you do during the day and how well you perform. Even procrastination is a habit that is built throughout the years, and it must be broken down and replaced with a new habit. Since habits are essential to success, we will go over some steps on creating new habits that you can help your client with.

Focus On One Habit at a Time

There is a term known as ego depletion which refers to a person's diminished capacity to regulate their emotions and actions. This phenomenon impedes our ability to form new habits because our willpower supply is spread out among all areas of our lives and there is only so much to go around. Therefore, trying to work on changing or creating multiple habits at once can seem impossible. This is why it's important to focus on one habit at a time. By doing this, your willpower will be channeled into focusing on one area, which will be more effective in the long run.

To increase the odds of success, choose one habit you want to focus on and learn everything you can do to it right. Since the focus of this book is business, we can help our clients determine what tendency is negatively impacting their business the most and work on correcting that. For example, if they are waking up late and don't have enough time to prepare for the day, we can help them work on changing this habit.

If your client thinks they have the willpower to change more than one habit at a time, they can certainly try. However, don't have them push it too much.

Commit to a Minimum of Thirty Days

There has been a lot of discussion on the amount of time it takes to officially turn a practice or routine. For example, how long will a person have to wake up by a certain time before it becomes natural? While the time frame can vary with every individual, a major consensus seems to be at least twenty-one days. This means you must perform a routine for twenty-one days straight before it can officially become a habit (Scott, 2016).

For this section, we will be extra cautious and give thirty days. When you are working with your client on developing their new habit, give them a timeframe of at least thirty days. At this point, you can assess and determine if more time is needed. Don't be too hung up on the length of time because the client should be allowed to move at their own pace. The timeline is just something to use as a reference.

. . .

Anchor the New Habit to an Established Habit

A new habit will be much easier to incorporate into a routine if it gets tied to an existing habit. For example, if you generally exercise every day, you can tell yourself that you will wake up earlier in the mornings to have more time for exercise. The following are some other examples:

- After I come home and change out of my work clothes, I will immediately change into my workout clothes and go for a run.
- After I get my kids ready for school, I will immediately plan my day ahead.

Anchor your habit to something you already do and it will become much easier to transition.

Take Baby Steps

You are not going to change overnight. There are very few instances of that actually happening. The only way to make a habit stick is by making it an automatic behavior that you perform naturally. You can get to this point by taking baby steps to create a new level of commitment. The objective is to create micro-commitments where it's nearly impossible to fail. If you want to wake up an hour earlier in the morning, start by making small milestones:

- Get up five minutes early on the first day with the goal of making it to twenty minutes by the end of the first week.
- Make a goal of reaching forty minutes by the end of week two.
- Your final goal will be to make sixty minutes by the end of week three.

These steps are simple, but they will require commitment. Keep doing them without missing a day.

Make a Plan for Obstacles

While you are creating a new habit or going after a goal, there will be plenty of obstacles along the way. While you cannot see all of them coming, you must prepare the best you can for most of them. Foresee potential obstacles that will come your way and do your best to plan for them. Examples of these include:

- Time
- Weather
- Other people
- Space
- Self-consciousness

Always anticipate obstacles and never assume it will be smooth sailing. Otherwise, you will be caught off guard constantly and this will be a major time-waster.

Create Accountability for Your Habit

When you create accountability for what you say, you are more likely to follow through on it. The great thing here is that your client will already have an accountability partner, and that is you as their coach. If a client knows you will be following up with them about what they've done as far as their habits, they are more likely to keep their goals.

You can also have your client find accountability partners in their personal lives, like friends or family members, to help them when you are not there.

Reward Important Milestones

Building a habit will take a lot of effort along the way. You will have a long road ahead and you should not wait until the end to reward yourself. You can give yourself rewards for smaller milestones along the way. This will help you to keep moving forward.

TIME IN TERMS OF PHILOSOPHY

We want to spend this section discussing the philosophy behind time and what it means to so many people. Many individuals in the modern world see time as money and if they are wasting it, they are essentially losing money. This can spill over into regretting time with family and friends or doing the thighs they love. During these moments, people who view time as money become angry, frustrated, or anxious because they are doing something that's not making them financially richer.

Unfortunately, when people live with this mindset, they are putting less value on their time because they are making a finite value out of it. Instead, people should see their time as priceless, since they have a limited amount of it that will never come back. Each second that passes, is a second that's gone for good. This is why it's so important to invest our time into a life that we get pleasure from. Yes, we need to work, and many of us want to accomplish great things while we are around. However, it is essential to use our minutes towards living a life we enjoy.

If people only look at time as a chance to make money, then anything they do outside of that realm will be a waste to them, and therefore, will never enjoy their present moment. Think of this example for a moment. You are sitting at a table with a good friend. You are there simply to relax and have a good conversation. However, your mind is preoccupied with the money you are not making while sitting at this table instead of working. As a result, you have wasted this precious time to talk to your friend. You can place yourself in any other situation and get similar feelings. How often do we hear stories about busy professionals who are too busy to spend time with their kids, spouses, or friends? These individuals are not too busy, they are just prioritizing work and money over valuable relationships.

From now on, ask yourself if you are using your time wisely. Are you enjoying it, investing it, and living the best life you can?

Are you simply focused on financial gain? If you thought about time as a finite resource that will soon be gone, would you use it differently? Think about this and determine where you want to go from here.

MANAGE YOUR TIME

Now that we have established the importance of time management, we will go over some essential time management techniques. In reality, we do not manage time because time keeps moving. We have no ability to stop it or slow it down. Plus, everybody has the same number of hours in a day. We are actually managing ourselves and what we are focusing our minds, actions, and energy towards.

The best time management techniques change the way we work, get rid of distractions, improve our concentration, and increase our overall productivity. There are numerous strategies floating around out there, but these are the ones we feel make the biggest difference.

Be Intentional By Keeping a To-Do List

While a to-do list is not a groundbreaking technique, it has been overlooked by many as an effective time management tool. Simply writing things down that need to get done can help ensure important tasks are not missed and we also save time trying to remember things. To-do lists can be broken down into different categories based on the type of tasks that need to be completed.

Having a list of tasks keeps you intentional on what you need to work on. By creating one, you are effectively laying out in words what needs to be completed. Never underestimate the power of writing things down. When your mind does wander, refer back to your list to keep yourself on track. As you complete items on your list, scratch them off so you don't have to wonder about them anymore.

There are many to-do list apps you can download. Also, you can use the old school pen-and-paper method. Whatever you don't get done on your list in one day, move over to the next. Just make sure the items you move are the less critical ones.

To-Do List

Prioritize Your Tasks

After writing out your to-do list, rank your tasks from highest priority to least priority and, of course, perform the higher priority tasks first. Doing this guides you through the activities of the day and ensures that the most critical tasks are taken care of. Prioritize what is important to you and not other people when making out your list.

Without prioritization, we often focus our attention on the wrong things in life. In addition, our attention goes towards pressing tasks that have a deadline, but we forget out the important projects too. Determine the tasks that will have the most positive effect on you, your work, and your team.

Manage Distractions

Distractions can come out of nowhere and get the best of all of us at some point. No matter how hard we try, distractions are unavoidable to a certain degree. We can be working hard and then decide to check emails or our social media accounts. Before we know it, more time has passed and we effectively became victims of a major distraction. Not only do we have to contend with the distraction itself, but also the time it takes to refocus on our original task, which can also be several minutes.

Distractions can come from many different sources and it's important to identify and eliminate them as much as possible during our working hours. Some common culprits include the aforementioned email and social media, television, background noise, phones and tablets, people, or anything in our environment that should not be there.

Timely is a great app for identifying and quantifying distractions. It can automatically record the time you spend on every work tool and website to see where all of your time is going. Apps like StayFocused or Mindful Browsing can put access restrictions on time-wasting websites. Also, log out of your emails, social media accounts, and other applications when you are not working on them. Disable popups or notifications. Keep your desk clear from anything that is not work-related. This includes snacks. If you get hungry, physically get up and eat. If snacks are close by, then you will be distracted much more often by taking small bites.

Distractions

Block Times For Your Work

Often, people work in small spurts between trying to take care of other activities like grocery shopping, picking up their kids, cooking dinner, or doing the laundry. However, to be the most effective with your time, you must block out certain portions of your schedule that will solely be dedicated to working. Time blocking protects your workspace and puts some healthy pressure on you to complete it.

Instead of juggling between many jobs, thinking you will get more done this way, focus on one job at a time. You will actually be more productive this way. There is a major myth out there about multitasking. People believe this is the only way to get everything done when in reality, less work is getting done and the outcomes are worse. This is because it is impossible to work on multiple things at the same time and still give each of them the same amount of focus.

Set aside time for administrative tasks too, like sending emails, filing, or making phone calls. These activities should not be part of your main workload.

Be Self-Aware and Track Your Time

Before you can start improving how you use your time, you need to understand how you use it in the first place. Tracking your time provides insights and self-awareness to make effective changes. When you perform this strategy, you become more aware of hidden items that drain your time and inefficient processes.

Fortunately, there are apps you can use to track your time to avoid having to do it manually. They will record your time and put it in a private timeline while you go about your day.

Employ some of these time management strategies with your clients to see how they work for them.

WHO ARE YOUR PROSPECTIVE CLIENTS?

A time management coach is along the same lines as a productivity coach. These types of coaches are essential in the business world because of the competitive nature and the need to get more work done in less time and with equal or greater results. Improving productivity will save companies a lot of time and money. Also, they will be putting out superior products and services in minimal amounts of time.

If you have the desire to become a productivity coach, you will be in high demand because you will be needed to guide organizations to achieve higher outputs without putting in the extra effort.

A good productivity coach is someone who can thoroughly guide their clients to work smart. By using the right tools, plus some logical and practical approaches to every activity, the coach can help their clients maximize results. As a coach in this sector, you will be able to observe your client's performance. You will be able to view their strengths and weaknesses. Finally, you will be able to help them simplify their daily routines, so they don't feel overwhelmed. If you are interested in all of this, then this line of coaching may be right up your alley. The following list summarizes what your role will entail.

- Supporting the client with a plan based on their goals.
- Helping define the objectives of a goal.

- Assisting clients in maintaining a work-life balance.
- Guiding clients on increasing sales and profits.

You will have plenty of business too once people become aware of your work. Many individuals in the business world become stressed and frustrated with all that they have going on and this severely affects their productivity and output. When you come in, you can help them develop better skills to improve their confidence, performance, and productivity. We will go over some of the prospective clients that you will have as a business coach.

Entrepreneurs

Entrepreneurs spend a lot of time on many different aspects of their business and mighty be doing everything themselves, especially if they are new. With all of the different responsibilities and distractions, they are bound to lose focus on their work which will severely reduce their output. A productivity coach will help them manage their time better. They can help entrepreneurs streamline their work, gain more clarity, and ultimately, increase their productivity.

Entrepreneurs are looking for ways to obtain better returns on investments. The tools provided by a productivity coach can help them implement the correct plans and strategies for higher profits. As a productivity coach, you will be very valuable to an entrepreneur.

Multinational Companies

Employees who work for multinational companies are always under a lot of pressure to show productivity. For their superiors, this is a measure of their worth to the company. Multinational companies need to get results, or they will cease to exist. For this to occur, they need a well-thought-out plan and a business coach is a perfect person to help them develop one.

A business coach can help these organizations by supporting them in finding solutions and achieving better sales results. Finally, a coach can provide the necessary tools that can develop various skills for a company's employees. This will help them with time management and effectively increase their productivity.

Educational Institutions

Educational institutions are always looking for ways to improve the productivity of their teaching staff and student body. These institutions want positive results from their students because it is a reflection on them too, and they also want to assess the effectiveness of their teaching methods. After analyzing the methods, coaches can train teaching staff in new skills and methods that will lead to students achieving better results on their exams and projects.

Time management and productivity are some of the most crucial skills to develop for success in the business world. You will help individuals greatly by focusing your efforts in these areas.

STEPS TO INCREASE PRODUCTIVITY

As a productivity coach, you can use certain steps to help improve your client's productivity. While you cannot tell your client what to do, you can certainly suggest some tips on how to increase productivity and overall performance. These traits will determine how much they actually get done toward setting up their business and other work. We will go over some simple strategies for productivity right here.

Schedule your work

Your clients can get into the habit of planning their work ahead of time. this means they should set aside 10-15 minutes every morning, or before they go to bed to plan out what their day will be like. This will eliminate the time wasted on wondering what needs to get done. Write it all done, prioritize, and follow the list you make.

Use Your Most Productive Hours Wisely

Many self-help gurus and even life coaches out there push the idea of waking up earlier to get more done. This strategy can work for some people, especially those who are early birds. However, the key to productivity is to use the hours in the day where you are most energetic and do as much of your important work as you can during these times. So, if you have more energy in the morning, wake up early and get your important work done then. If you are a night owl, then stay up late working and completing important tasks. If you get energy in the afternoon, take advantage of these hours.

Help your client figure out what hours of the day they work best in. Encourage them to take advantage of these productive hours by doing as much as they can.

Organize Life on a Weekly Basis

Plan out your week on Sunday night. You don't have to have everything written down since you will still be making daily lists, but you should have a general idea of what your week will look like. In doing this, the client will have a sense of what steps they will take when on their most vital projects.

Treat All Days as Special

Every day of the week should be treated as special, even if it's a day meant for relaxation. Use the following list as an example:

- Sunday: Plan the week ahead.
- Monday: Work on Budgeting.
- Tuesday: Update marketing plan.
- Wednesday: Plan for any meetings or conferences.
- Thursday: Order inventory.
- Friday: Stock inventory.
- Saturday: Relaxation day.

Have a Review at the End of Each Day

When your day is all said and done, sit down and review what you were able to do and if you met all of your goals. If not, see where you need to make some changes.

Productivity is an essential part of running a business and a productivity coach can be essential in making a difference for the client.

4

MARKETING COACHING

Starting and building up a business is tedious work that often seems never-ending. There are many unanswered questions and several uncertainties on the horizon. Starting a business is a big risk and you have the potential to create something big or fail badly. Up to this point, we have discussed the benefits of having a business coach to help us develop a business plan from start to finish and manage our time properly. Another major aspect of running a business is marketing. Without a good marketing plan, your business will be lucky to get off the ground because no one will know that it exists.

Marketing is very tricky, especially with the advent of so many platforms and various techniques to get your post shown on various websites. As a business owner, many try their hand at this process without having to understand what SEO content means or what click funnels are. Marketing has become a science and the days of putting an ad in the local paper are a thing of the past.

Since marketing is quite complicated yet very important for a business, a marketing coach can be an essential partner in getting your business' name out there.

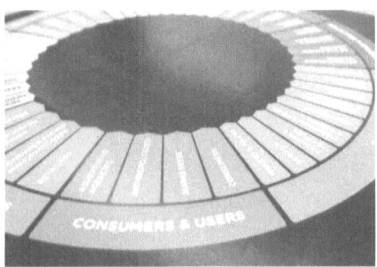
Marketing

WHO IS A MARKETING COACH?

A marketing coach is someone who works with business owners and managers to develop strategies with the goal being an increase in revenue without the business owner putting in extra time for marketing. Whether a business wants to increase its online sales or reach a broader segment of the market, a marketing coach will have the knowledge and skills to create an action plan for both.

Since proper marketing is vital to the success of a business, the skills of a marketing catch can be invaluable. What are some of the specific ways a coach can help in this sector? The following are a few examples:

- Helping the business owner stay focused on the remainder of the important business processes.
- Eliminating many of the errors during the marketing process so that less effort, money, and time get wasted.
- Implementing efficient and effective marketing strategies to obtain superior outcomes quickly.
- Helping avoid the shiny objects, or "magic bullets" that will supposedly revolutionize the way marketing is done. There are many scams out there that promise the world when you engage in certain marketing strategies. A good marketing coach can be there to identify these scams and sift them out.
- Developing long-term plans for marketing that will continuously help the business grow.

A good marketing coach can also guide a business owner at when, why, and how a specific marketing tool should be used. For example, they can decide to:

- Redesign a website
- Start a business blog
- Go on a podcast or start a podcast
- Engage in social media or LinkedIn marketing

With a marketing coach by your side, you will have less anxiety when trying to find ways to promote your business.

. . .

Characteristics of a Marketing Coach

While marketing coaches can come from all different backgrounds and have specific skill sets, there are three essential characteristics that all marketing coaches must possess. These traits are the foundation of how they approach their client's needs.

- Empathy for the clients. This means there is an emotional connection and the coach is able to feel what their clients are going through. This is almost like walking in a person's shoes.
- An unwavering curiosity to hone their marketing skills. Marketing trends are continuously changing and a good coach will always keep up on the trends, tools, and ideas that are bringing in the best results.
- The ability to influence their clients through effective communication, management, and leadership skills.

A Good Marketing Plan

Just like any other business, a coach should not spend a dime on marketing until they have a solid plan to figure out what they are doing. Otherwise, you are just throwing your money at the wall and seeing if it sticks. As a business owner, you must value money because it can be hard to come by in many instances. Many coaches out there start up their practice without having any idea how they will generate leads or attract new clients. Therefore, they will not gain any business or make profits.

Create a solid marketing plan to help your business flourish. Your marketing plan must clearly state who you will be targeting with your services. For example, are you going to be a general business coach or get more specific into the subsets like a productivity or time management coach? Do you plan to work with a particular age group, as adults in their twenties, a certain gender, or people with specific socioeconomic backgrounds? Your marketing plan must also identify how you plan on finding clients and what you will need to do to make all of this happen.

Businesses generally fail because they don't have a steady stream of customers. This is because they fail to plan in so many ways, including their marketing. If you have a unique understanding of marketing or like to help a specific type of business, becoming a marketing coach can be a great option for you. You will have many potential clients including:

- Small business owners
- Managing directors/CEOs
- Small to medium enterprises (SMEs)
- Large organizations
- Marketing teams
- Entrepreneurs of all kinds

WHY DO BUSINESSES HIRE A MARKETING COACH?

A marketing coach can be a great investment for any type of business, whether large or small. No matter what sector or industry you are in, potential customers and clients must know that you exist. Proper marketing is essential for this to occur. Therefore, a great marketing coach can be worth their weight in gold. As a marketing coach yourself, you will be highly valuable to all types of business owners.

Small Businesses

A business that is in the initiation phases may not have the budget or finances available to test out various marketing strategies. The last thing you want to do as a new business owner is to throw money away on things that don't work. What will work is finding a high-quality coach who can guide you in the right direction. A good marketing coach will combine the ideas and passions of the business owner with their own unique marketing strategies to build an effective action plan for success.

Many techniques, tools, and programs, will help boost growth for your small business. The following are some special ways that a marketing coach can help:

- The coach will guide them in not short-selling themselves. Business owners have the right to charge what their product or service is worth, so don't sell

yourself short in this regard. A good coach can help you determine what you're selling is worth so they don't underprice themselves.
- The coach will help a business find their ideal clients. This will definitely help you generate some leads.
- The coach will also guide a business owner on how to be prepared when their business starts to ramp up. The coach will make sure the owner is not overwhelmed and continue to remain afloat.

New small business owners are naive to many things and no matter how many books you read or seminars you attend, you will be bombarded with many different issues. These will be enough to bring anyone down, and that is why so many business owners fail. A marketing coach can help you keep your business running strong. They will have your back through good and bad times.

Big Businesses

Some businesses have been around for many years and their situation is much different than a new business owner. For experienced business owners, the entrepreneurial spark is often gone or diminished. They get bored and let their guard down. What they need in times like these are new marketing strategies that will make their businesses thrive again. Many of these owners have not kept up with the latest marketing platforms and are still stuck in the old school methods.

A marketing coach can help such businesses and their owners remain on par with their competition by staying up to date on new marketing techniques. The coach will guide the business owners on how to leverage current marketing platforms which can be very complicated.

Any size business can benefit from the wisdom, connections, and experience of a marketing coach. The following are some of the sectors a coach should have a command of that a business owner can look for:

- Management
- Creating operational systems
- Marketing and Finance
- Developing sales
- Merchandising for retail
- Training employees

Of course, the main reason for hiring a coach is to help create a marketing plan that will succeed. No matter what kind of business it is, like an online, physical store, food, clothing, industrial, or anything else, you need to craft a winning marketing message and an ultimate client profile.

A marketing message will be the first thing your client's main audience will notice. You need to make a good first impression. To make a great client profile, focus on industries where you feel the most comfortable. For example, if you are more familiar with the retail and food industry, you should stick to these areas at first and avoid corporate businesses. Do this at least at the very beginning until you gain more experience. As a coach, to make a marketing plan work, you must focus on the following:

- Get in-depth knowledge of the actual business for which the marketing plan needs to be built around. Understand everything you can about the business, including all goals and needs.
- Don't try to experiment with all of the marketing strategies out there. Instead, trust the platforms and ways that you think will bring the most return on investment. For instance, LinkedIn marketing might be more effective for corporate businesses than Facebook or Instagram marketing, whereas Instagram might be the best for creative pathways, like art, painting, or photography.
- Always take your client's budget into account. You do not want to run them dry trying to market their business. Assess what your client has and what they are willing to spend on marketing. Do not create your plan until you analyze the financial position of your client. For a startup business, you may need to focus on more organic marketing techniques, rather than paid. Bigger businesses with larger budgets will likely go for paid marketing strategies.
- Create short-term marketing plans and move on. Your

marketing efforts will need time to build up and won't show results all at once. Always include small, actionable steps in your plan and have SMART goals.

SPECIFIC MARKETING STRATEGIES

For the final section of this chapter, we will describe some common marketing strategies to give you an idea of what direction you can take.

Building a Website

With everything being on the internet these days, it is hard to imagine a business not having a website or some type of online presence. A good website that is eye-catching is the most important ingredient for efficient marketing. It makes it possible for people all over the world to find you. As a marketing coach, you must be aware of how to drive traffic back to a website using innovative techniques. This includes designing websites that attract clients, click funnels, and SEO content. You must have a thorough knowledge of content marketing basics and how to generate leads for your client through their website.

Even the smallest businesses out there have websites or a web presence through social media. It's hard to run a business of any kind without one, so if your client is not at this level yet, it could be a recommendation that needs to be made.

Website Marketing

Promo-Kit

A promo-kit is also a great marketing technique to get people to view your work. It might seem obsolete to a certain degree since everything can be found online, but a good promo-kit can still hold some value. The following are some items to keep together for this tool:

- Audiotaped and videos
- Articles
- Media quotes or mentions
- Brochures
- Resumes
- Headshots

Classified Ads

Classified ads are low-cost and a great way to market yourself on a regular basis. You can use these types of ads to offer free sessions, products, articles, and other items related to your client's business.

Newsletters

Newsletters have become an old school method of marketing, but they are still very relevant today. A newsletter can be used to pass along a lot of valuable information about a business and the products or services they provide. As a marketing coach, it is important to learn how you can utilize newsletters for the benefit of your client's business.

Referrals

A marketing coach can guide their clients on how to increase their referral flow. This is similar to word-of-mouth marketing which is still one of the most effective methods. People who had a good experience with you telling other people are still marketing gold. Building a channel of new clients from existing ones demands much effort. With smart strategies, this can attract many clients. To get a proper referral flow, you must find a good balance between being too pushy and being too passive.

Press Releases

Press releases can greatly enhance the media presence of a business owner. As a marketing coach, this will be a big boost for your client. Press releases take a certain amount of skill and they can lead to more print media, radio or podcast interviews, and the chance to be shown on television.

. . .

Free Offerings

You might be wondering why free offerings should be given as you are trying to make money. However, this is a great marketing technique that tells your client you believe in your product or service. For example, you can give away free samples, or offer webinars and event workshops.

These various marketing strategies will work best based on what your goals are and what particular business you belong to. As a marketing coach, you can determine what techniques work best for your clients.

COMPLEMENTING WITH A BLOG

To help complement their coaching business, many individuals set up a blog where they write articles full of useful information. Potential clients find blogs very attractive because of how informative they are. A blog can be a small section of a website or a web page all on its own. Not only is blogging a great educational tool, but can help market too. Furthermore, once you learn how to set up a good blog, you can help your clients create one for their own businesses too.

A blog has to do three things:

- Acquire leads: These are from your readers who have an interest in your product or service.

- Nurture sales: Makes your prospects more likely to visit your sales page.
- Retain your customers: Helps to build up brand loyalty. When your clients feel like you add value to their lives, they tend to stay with you for the long haul.

The following are some of the key reasons why you should start a business blog:

- Drive more traffic to your website. Business blogging allows you to create great resources in the form of articles or posts that your prospective clients are looking for. These resources can include:
- Guides that completely cover a topic from start to finish.
- "How-to" articles that describe how to overcome some sort of challenge. For example, as a business coach, you can write a short "how-to" article on time management.
- A checklist with action steps to complete a task.
- Improve the search ranking for your website. When your prospects are searching online, they will be typing in some keywords. When you blog, you are bound to use some keywords related to your industry. The more often you blog, the higher the chances of your keywords and content being discovered.
- Build more readership and stronger relationships with

your customers. When people see you active online, they are more likely to engage with you. They will get to know you on a more intimate level too, which will help you sell your products or services. Blogging will provide a great connection between you and your customers, which will foster loyalty.
- Establish you and your brand as an industry leader. This relates to gaining credibility. If you regularly put out helpful and engaging content, clients will see you as more knowledgeable.
- It is very inexpensive to start and easy to set up. All you really need is a hosting website like WordPress or Weebly, which is very cheap. These hosting sites are also user friendly.
- Spur interactions with other industry leaders and prospective clients, especially when they start commenting on your posts. These types of engagements allow you to:
- Address any questions or concerns that prospects might have.
- Gain new topic ideas to research and write about.
- Get to know other bloggers and industry leaders.
- Helps nurture prospects towards an easier sale. The more content clients read about a product or service, the more likely they are to purchase it. Therefore, the more quality blogs you write, the easier it will be to make sales.

As your blog gets bigger, you can add followers, subscribers, and even people who want to pay for advertising on your site. It can become a side business on its own. With a blog, it's important to get it known, as well, by sharing it through multiple platforms. Other options that work in a similar fashion can be YouTube videos, podcasts, or social media groups. A blog is still easier to set up than YouTube or podcasts because certain equipment is needed, but these other choices have gotten simpler too.

There are many marketing options out there, so help clients find the best ones for them.

5

COMMON BUSINESS COACHING QUESTIONS

One of the most important items a coach will have in their arsenal is their ability to ask effective questions. This does not just mean asking the right questions, but also when to ask them and what tone to use. In many cases, it is not what you say, it is how you say it.

A conversation between a coach and a client rarely follows a perfect sequential path. However, by using the GROW model, a business coach can set up a nice framework to help structure their coaching sessions. Several managers of big companies have used the GROW Model with their employees as well. GROW stands for:

- Goal
- Reality (Current Reality)
- Options

- Will

It can be used by coaches and managers alike to improve performance, solve problems, make better and more informed decisions, learn new skills, and reach desired career goals.

The key to using the GROW models is to ask exceptional questions. The objective is not to tell people what to do, but to ask what is best for them. As a coach, it is your job to help clients come up with answers on their own through strategic questioning methods. think of yourself as a private investigator who is asking many followup questions until everyone has arrived at an answer. The GROW model is also a great way for new coaches to get used to asking appropriate questions. With experience, it will eventually become natural and automatic.

Questions=Answers

DISSECTING THE GROW MODEL

We will get more in-depth with the GROW Model and provide greater detail into what each step means. Within each step are specific questions you can ask the client.

Goal

Establishing a goal is the first step in the coaching process. This will lay the foundation for where the business coach and client will go. Goals can be categorized as performance goals, development goals, a problem that needs to be solved, important decisions to be made, or a goal just for a specific coaching session. Whenever you are discussing a goal with your clients, encourage them to make SMART goals, which stands for:

- Specific
- Measurable
- Attainable
- Realistic
- Timely

If a goal covers all of these factors, then it will be concrete and real. If you want to obtain financing for a business, a good goal statement can be: "I will be visiting at least five financial institutions this week to determine which one will give the best deal on interest rates and I plan to open a business loan by Friday that will cover my initial business expenses." This is a better statement than: "I want a million dollar loan to open a business." There is nothing really concrete about the second statement.

To help people gain clarity about their goals and make sure you're both on the same page, use the following questions:

- That specific goal do you want to achieve during this coaching session?
- What do you REALLY want right now?
- What overall goal do you want to achieve?
- What do you want to accomplish?
- What results do you want to accomplish?
- What is your ideal end result?
- What do you want to change the most?
- Why are you hoping to obtain this goal?
- What benefits would you obtain from accomplishing this goal?

Current Reality

This step in the GROW Method is to realize what your current situation is. Determine what is happening in your life, why it is happening, the context in which it is taking place, and the magnitude of the whole situation. During this step, the client needs to have time to think and reflect so they get the full scope of what is happening. The coach must display patience and allow their client the opportunity to really think everything through. This does not have to be a rapid-fire interrogation process.

Instead, ask appropriate questions and then sit back and wait for the response. Do not share your opinion or offer solutions. Just pay attention to your active listening skills. Get a clear understanding of your client's current reality with the following questions:

- What is happening to you now? What is the effect it is having?
- What steps have you taken towards your goal already if any?
- What is the best way to describe what you did?
- Where are you now in relation to where you want to be? How much further do you need to go?
- Where do you find yourself on a scale from 1-10?
- Regarding the success you have had so far, what do you feel is the largest contributor?
- What progress have you made thus far?
- What are you doing right now that is working well for you?
- What is required of you to reach your outcomes?
- What has stopped you from reaching your goal already?
- Do you know that other people have achieved similar goals to you?
- What have you already tried doing?

- What could you do better this time than in the past?
- On a scale of 1-10, how urgent is this situation?
- If you asked your friends what they think, what would they say about you?

Options

The third leg of the GROW Method is options. During this process, we help the client determine what they can do to reach their goals. The following questions will help your clients explore their options and generate solutions:

- What are all of your options?
- What do you believe you need to do next?
- What is a possible first step?
- What action do you think you need to take to achieve better results and get closer to your goal?
- What else could you do right now?
- Who else can help you with your goals?
- If you decided to do nothing, what would happen?
- What has already worked for you in your life? How can you do more of what worked?
- If you did more of what worked, what would happen?
- What is the most challenging part of that for you?
- What advice would you give to a friend about that?
- What would you gain or lose by saying or doing that?
- If someone did or said that to you what do you think would happen?

- What is the best/worst thing about this option?
- Which option out there are you ready to act on now?
- When you were in a similar situation before, how did you handle it?
- What things can you do differently now?
- Who out there has encountered a similar situation that you know of?
- If anything in the world was possible, and money or failure was not a factor, what would you do?
- What other options can you think of?

Will

This is the final portion of the GROW Method. The coach's job is to check for commitment and guide their clients in establishing a clear action plan. The following are some questions to help you search for and achieve commitments:

- How are you going to go about your goal?
- What actions do you need to take right now?
- How are you going to do that?
- How will you know when you have done it?
- What else can you do?
- What is the chance of your plan succeeding on a scale of 1-10?
- What is blocking your success right now?
- What other roadblocks are expected along the way?
- What resources exist that can help you?

- What is missing?
- What one small step can you take at this time?
- At what point are you going to start?
- When you reach success, what will that look like for you?
- What support systems do you need to reach this success you are imagining?
- What will happen if you don't take these actions?
- What do you need from others, including me, to help you achieve this?
- What are three sensible actions you can take this week towards your success?
- On a scale of 1-10, how committed are you to do what you say?
- What would it take to make your scale reach 10?

The GROW Method is a great way to get inside your client's mind and find out what they really want in their lives. the best part is, you don't have to tell them as they will slowly come to a realization on their own. If you noticed, there were very few, if any, "yes" or "no" questions. These are something you want to avoid because they can close off a conversation right away. Instead, focus on open-ended questions which will lead to follow-up questions based on your client's answers.

Growth

Business Focused Questions

To round out this chapter, we will go over some business-related questions using the GROW Method. As a business coach, you can ask your clients these questions to help them, and their businesses, grow. Once again, these questions are a great way to start a coaching and client session:

- What do you want your business to be known for? If someone were to write an article or film about it, what would they write?
- At its peak, what is your business like?
- What is the most important thing personally about what you do?
- What specific things does your business do really well?
- What is dissatisfying to you at the moment?
- If you could go back to the beginning of the year, or at least several months, what business advice would you give yourself?

- When your customers or competitors look at your business, what do they see?
- When you look at the progress of your business up to this point, on a scale of 1-10, how satisfied are you?
- If your satisfaction rating is not at a ten, what do you need to get it there?
- Looking forward to the next Christmas, imagine yourself being extremely excited by all of your accomplishments. As you look back, what would you have achieved to create this excitement?
- Over the next six months, what are three words that sum up your ideal self-image as a business owner?

Remember that your skills at asking questions can make or break a coaching session.

QUESTIONING TECHNIQUES

> *"The answers you get depend on the questions you ask."*
>
> — THOMAS KUHN

The above quote is definitely astute because if you want certain types of answers, you must ask certain types of questions. The questions you ask will not only lead to the information you get but also the relationships you develop. It will also help you avoid misleading people which is very important for you as a business coach.

In this section, we will review some of the everyday types of questions people ask and the responses they are likely to elicit.

Closed Questions

These are the types of questions we generally avoid during a coaching session. They generally invite one-word answers and limit following up questions. Of course, you can also swerve back around and keep questioning your clients, even after asking closed questions. If it only requires a "yes" or "no answer, it is considered a closed question. These are great for breaking the ice. For example, you can ask someone you just met if they are doing okay today. Also, if you want a quick answer, these questions will be useful at that time, as well. Once again, these will rarely be used in a coaching session where a relationship needs to be developed.

Open Questions

Open-ended questions require a lot more thought and are generally followed by a longer response. Some examples would be:

- Where do you see yourself in ten years?
- What are the best options you see for yourself moving forward?

These types of questions leave room for proper follow-up and keep the conversation moving forward. These are the perfect types of questions for a coaching session.

Probing Questions

These questions are great for gaining some clarification about what was said and encourages others to share more information. Probing questions usually come in a series that digs deeper into a situation and provide a larger picture of what is going on. For example, you can ask someone, "How soon do you want to get started, what topics do you want to discuss, and how long do you want our meeting to be?" Based on the responses, you can ask further probing questions. Probing questions are great to help avoid misunderstandings and gain more information from people who are reluctant.

Leading Questions

Leading questions are designed to lead an individual down a certain route, whether positive or negative. As a coach, your goal will be to lead them down a positive route. These types of questions can be helpful or manipulative, depending on how they are approached. Examples of leading questions and how they can be veered towards the negative or positive are as follows:

- *"Are there any issues with taking on this project?"*
- *"Are you happy to take on this project?"*

As you can see, the second question slightly leads a person towards the positive. Leading questions can also be used to coerce people into agreeing with a speaker. For example, a business coach can ask one of their clients, "This coaching session is going great, isn't it?" In a subtle way, the coach is almost forcing the client to answer in a certain way. A more appropriate question would be, "How are you feeling about this coaching session?" This is simple and unassuming.

A leading question can be used to build a positive discussion, which is good for a coaching session, or trying to steer the conversation towards an outcome that serves you, which is something you need to avoid in a coaching session. Avoid using leading questions as an unfair way to get what you want.

Loaded Questions

These questions are pretty straightforward and appear as closed questions, but come with a twist: They contain an assumption about the respondent. Some examples would be:

- Have you stopped drinking?
- Did you smoke your last cigarette this week?

- Are you going to revert back to your old habits?

Since the coaching and client relationship cannot work off of assumptions and finger-pointing, loaded questions should be avoided. Save these for when people are getting interrogated.

Funnel Questions

These questions begin broadly and then narrow up to a specific point, just like a funnel. They can also go in the opposite direction. When we meet someone new, we generally start with narrower questions and then broaden them out into more open-ended questions. For instance, you will ask someone their names during a first meeting and start asking broader questions to get more information.

In the reverse, broad questions are asked when more general information is needed and as we achieve it, we can slowly narrow things down to obtain more exact information. Funnel questions can be used to diffuse tension. For example, asking someone broad questions about an issue can distract them from their anger and gives you more information to help them find a solution.

Overall, funnel questions are great for developing relationships, discovering specific information, and diffusing arguments.

Rhetorical Questions

These types of questions don't really require an answer. They are more like phrases or statements disguised as questions so the conversation is more engaging for the listener. They can be used by coaches to get their clients to spur thoughts and ideas.

The Tone of a Question

In addition to the type of question to be asked, the tone is also important. This includes quality of voice, body language, and facial expressions. The tone of a question can completely alter the meaning, even if the same words are used. For example, a sarcastic tone will come off differently than a warm and friendly tone.

The matriculation of technology has thrown a wrench into the situation, as well. With the advent of emojis and gifs, new ways of reading messages have been born. As a coach, you always want to make sure you are conveying the right message with your tone. Always use techniques for clarification to make sure there are no misunderstandings.

6

TOP CORE BUSINESS COACHING SKILLS

Coaching has slowly risen to become a practice of helping people learn, but not telling them what to do. Instead, a coach helps people find the right answers within themselves which is where the best solutions come from. As a result of helping people make their own decisions, coaches can truly lead people into reaching their full potential.

A good coach will help their clients break down the barriers that are getting in their way. In most cases, the barrier is their own mind. The foundational belief in the coaching profession is that the client always has the answers to their problems, no matter how great they might be. They just need a little guidance along the way, and the coach can work as their roadmap or GPS. Therefore, the responsibility ultimately lies on the client, which means they can walk away knowing they have the capability to change their lives and that is very empowering.

Of course, this does not mean that the coach does not have any culpability. A good coach will know that they are responsible for making sure they give their best to their clients. A good coach never shows disinterest, assumes, judges, or dismisses their clients' feelings among other things. Most importantly coaches bring a certain set of skills to the table. These are part of their arsenal to give their clients the best of who they are.

COACHING SKILLS

Just because coaching is still largely an unregulated profession, does not mean you do not need excessive knowledge and training to be the best. You absolutely do because if you try to go in cold, you are setting yourself, and your clients, up for failure. This is definitely not fair to those who seek your help. The most important aspect of becoming a great business coach is the skills you develop to help others become the best versions of themselves.

The three core coaching skills are listening, thinking, and speaking. Coaches do these things differently than anyone else. When they listen, they try to really hear what the client is saying. What are their hopes and aspirations? What are their strengths and weaknesses? What are they really interested in? What things in life do they fear the most? What areas of their life is the client trying to avoid? Which aspects of their life do the clients seem fixated on? What is not being said during the session? Are there any inconsistencies in what the client is saying? A coaching session goes well beyond a regular discussion. The coach must actively listen for even the smallest clues that can lead the conversation into many different directions.

The next core is thinking. Thinking like a coach is much different than just thinking in the general sense. Coaches think in terms of now. Whatever happened in the past is not of great importance. Even if the coach and client relationship has been going on for a while, the main thing the coach has on their mind is what value they can bring to their client in that very moment they are with them, whether it is an actual session, a phone conference, or any other official interaction.

The final core skill is speaking. The way a coach speaks is also unique. When you are talking to someone in a conversation, their response to you is that of giving advice or their opinion. You are probably the same way when answering a person back. For a coach, speaking is done in the service of others. This means they do not speak to look good, feel good, or show how intelligent they are. The sole purpose of speaking is to serve their client.

While these are the core coaching skills, there are many more that we will get into while also providing greater details. Remember that without your coaching skills, you will not help your clients reach their potential. It is necessary to learn these methods for the sake of the clients you will work with in the future.

Listening

We touched upon the coaching skill of listening already but want to get into more depth because of how important it is. It is probably the most essential skill to possess as a coach because if you cannot listen well, you will not understand your client's needs and will not be able to respond appropriately. This is why we put this skill at the top of the list. This does not just mean listening to what is said, but what is not being said. A good coach must learn to read between the lines of a conversation. This is where some of the most important information is discovered.

This is where a coach can ask really insightful questions of their clients to determine what is going on. We discussed the GROW Model and how essential it is for asking appropriate questions. Always remember this technique when moving forward to get the most information about your client. Through the GROW Model, there are four levels of listening skills:

- Attentive listening: This is when you give someone your full attention without distractions or letting your mind wander. When someone is speaking to you, listen to them fully.
- Accurate listening: Completely understanding the issue at hand. If you do not understand it, then ask appropriate follow-up questions until you do.
- Empathetic listening: Listening and showing complete

appreciation of the person's feelings concerning the issue at hand. This is done without judgment. To listen empathetically, you must leave your own vantage point and put yourself in the other person's shoes.
- Generative listening: Once again, completely understanding the issues at hand which allows you to ask insightful questions based on what the person needs.

Questioning

After listening to someone appropriately, you must then be able to ask great questions which is at the heart of great coaching. There are so many types of questions we can use and we used numerous examples in chapter five. As you gain more experience as a coach, you will pick up on many more subtle clues that will lead you to ask specific questions.

Some questions are more helpful than others, even within the same coaching session, but the best ones give insight into who the client really is. Questions must be open-ended so that appropriate follow-up can be conducted at all times. In most cases, it takes multiple questions to find a real solution, so avoid asking anything that will close off a conversation immediately.

The best way to stick with open-ended questions is to think about the "5 Bums on a Rugby Post" method. Each bum makes the shape of a "W" and the rugby post has the "H" shape. For those of you who don't understand this reference, it means that each question should begin with one of the five "W" words: What, where, who, why, or when. Or, it can start with the "H" word, which is how. In a pure coaching scenario, only open-ended questions starting with these types of words are used.

One of the best tips for asking good questions is to play off your own curiosity. Be curious about your client and look at the process of gaining information as a treasure hunt. Do not stop asking questions until you find that magic solution or treasure. Once you do, ask some more.

Building Rapport

Chronologically speaking, this is the first skill you will need when you start working with any client in order for the relationship to move forward. In fact, you will need to build rapport beforehand because your clients need to trust you prior to working with you in the first place. If you do not create rapport right from the beginning, the remainder of the coaching process will not work. Even if a client chooses to be a part of some sessions, they will never open up fully. This will be a major problem in the long run.

The rapport should also be maintained throughout the relationships so the coach and client will continue to work well together. Rapport is what allows coachees to be relaxed and to become vulnerable. This is where the greatest truths are revealed and personal barriers and fears are identified. Having good rapport also allows the coach to ask more difficult and insightful questions.

Some of the key factors in creating rapport include:

- Having empathy, or the ability to see the other person's point of view. We will get into more detail about this later.
- Having the right body language portrays a welcoming tone. For example, it is better to sit forward in a chair and look like you're attuned with the client, than sitting with our back against a chair with your arms folded. The latter will make it seem like you are not engaged whatsoever. You can also match and mirror your client's body language.
- Being warm and personable. Instead of sitting right across from someone, sit at more of an angle.
- Using the right tone of voice and language.

It is easier to build rapport with someone who appears honest and interested from the beginning. An important thing to note is that the coaching and client connection is similar to other types of relationships in that you will not always click with everybody. For whatever reason, you will not be able to coach certain people, not because you aren't good at it, but because the dynamics are not compatible. Sometimes, two people are like oil and water and there is nothing that can be done about it.

Always give it the college try and put in your best effort as a coach. However, when it becomes apparent that progress is not being made, it is better to cut things off respectfully and go in separate directions. If possible, you can certainly assist the client in finding a more compatible coach.

Having a good rapport with clients leads directly to successful coaching sessions.

Rapport

Empathizing

Empathy is defined as the ability to put ourselves in other people's shoes so we can get a perspective from their point of view. Often, it is hard to imagine why someone would make certain decisions or think a particular way. When we show empathy, we are more likely to appreciate their feelings and behavior in any given situation. As a coach, you will understand what it feels like to be your client.

Empathy is one of the most important people skills to have. It is essential for good communication and to remember that our focus should not be on what we would do in a situation, but what is best for that particular person to do. Empathy is such a forgotten skill because people are overly focused on themselves.

The goal of empathy is to help you understand the needs of another person. This is exceptionally important when building rapport in a coaching relationship. The client must feel like you are trying to understand them. When they realize this, they will be much more forthcoming with their personal information.

Empathy is often confused with sympathy, but it is not the same thing. Sympathy is simply feeling compassion for the hardship a person is going through, whereas empathy means you become one with the person going through the distress. Sometimes, you can actually feel what they feel during the most extreme forms of empathy. Both of these qualities are great to have in the coaching profession but empathy definitely takes it a step further.

Summarizing and Reflecting

These two skills help guide your client in making sense of what they are grappling with. Summarizing means you are repeating a condensed version of what the client said. With this process, you take the main point of their message and reiterate them. This will allow the client to make any corrections about what was understood by the coach and make sure everyone is on the same page. In addition, summarizing keeps the client focused on the topic at hand so continued progress can be made. As a coach, it's important to use this summarizing technique to reduce any chances of miscommunication. If you are unsure of what the client said, don't hesitate to ask them as many follow-up questions as needed.

Reflecting is another strategy where the coach paraphrases what their coachee said in order to show comprehension. This is an effective skill that can reinforce the thoughts of the client. The coach will also be able to step back and look at what was said objectively. Both of these techniques will ensure proper and clear communication is taking place between the coach and client.

Unlocking Limiting Beliefs

Many clients that you work with have not realized their goals because they do not believe in themselves enough. They are halted by their limiting beliefs and you have the opportunity to help them overcome these barriers of the mind. Beliefs are a principle that is automatically accepted as true without any real proof. Therefore, a person who believes they are not good enough, smart enough, or talented enough has a mindset that's not rooted in any facts. The only reason they have limiting beliefs is that they are too hard on themselves. Perhaps past failures are plaguing their mind, but the past should not predict the future.

Our beliefs have a significant impact on our behavior, which ultimately decide our results. Some beliefs make us successful, while others hold us back. Limiting beliefs can make people feel trapped. Where do these limitations come from, there can be a variety of sources, like past failures, the environment, how people were treated as children, and the support system they have now.

As a coach, helping your clients identify the underlying causes of their limiting beliefs and then challenge them is one of the most powerful coaching processes there can be. This process can be extremely emotional and enlightening for the client, and you, as the coach, will play a major role. Once again, you are not telling them what their limiting beliefs are, but guiding them into finding their own answers and solutions. Your role will be to get the other person to question their inner beliefs. It might be something they have never done before, so expect a little bit of pushback. However, if you have built up some rapport as we discussed earlier, you will have a better chance of getting through.

Staying Focused

When we are just talking in general conversation, it is not unusual to veer off track and discuss many different topics. During a session, it is important for a coach to make sure everything stays on track. The conversation must be focused on finding answers to the client's particular problems and not degenerate into just a regular discussion. Also, do not digress by getting into too much detail. We are not saying you can't be friendly and have some fun with your client, but do not lose sight of the goal.

To remain focused, you can use many of the techniques already described, like the GROW Model, asking appropriate questions, and summarizing. You may also need to interject once in a while to pull the conversation back to the center. Allow your client the freedom to express themselves, but do not allow them to completely go off the rails. There are still problems that need solutions.

Being Non-Judgemental and Open-Minded

When you judge someone, you have already made up your mind about who they are and what they are capable of. A coach is supposed to help their clients realize their own potential and live without limits. This is why it's critical to be non-judgemental. As a coach, you do not get to judge another human being. You must maintain your curiosity and remain open-minded to all of the possibilities the client will come up with. Being open minded means being empathetic too. This gives you the ability to view the world through their prism. From their vantage point, their views may be the right ones for them.

Open-minded

Resisting the Temptation to Tell

Being a coach is different than being a consultant or mentor. This is why you must never tell the client what to think. It can be very tempting to do so because humans like to solve other people's problems. It makes them feel good. However, that is not the purpose of coaching. The client has the best outcomes and will remain accountable when they are allowed to come up with their own solutions. In the end, they will appreciate it more too. Always resist the temptation to tell or give advice.

Give Constructive Feedback

The great thing about being a coach is that you can provide an outside perspective for someone that is objective since you don't have a personal connection. As a coach, you will be in a privileged position to point out certain things you notice about your clients, like their behaviors, facial expressions, reactions to specific questions, or body language during certain moments. Of course, keep these observations non-judgemental. For example, you can simply point out that they smile when certain words are spoken and become closed off with other words.

In most cases, your feedback will be well received by your client, especially if you have developed a rapport. It is pretty apparent that not much can be accomplished without rapport from the beginning. When you are giving feedback, make sure it is the following:

- Motivating
- Honest and from the heart
- Empathetic
- Timely
- Specific
- Balanced
- Actionable

There is a major difference between feedback and criticism. Do not tell a person something just for the heck of it. Point it out should be helpful to them in some way.

There are many coaching skills that you must develop before you are able to help your clients. They will seek you out for help, so you must do as much as you can to guide them towards success. Clients will have many fears and concerns when they are going into business. Having a good relationship with a business can make all the difference in the world.

INCREASING EMPATHY

Since empathy is such an important skill to have in order to really put your clients first, We will discuss some action steps you can take to increase your empathy. With empathy, you are able to understand another person's feelings and emotions because you are partly sharing them. You can feel what they are going through, which makes you more helpful in guiding them towards solutions. People who lack empathy are viewed as cold, self-absorbed, and uncaring. To become a good coach, you want to avoid getting this type of reputation. Remember that a client can only know what you show them. If you show them disinterest, whether it's true or not, then they will never be fully vulnerable with you.

Empathy is partly innate and partly learned. This means that some people are naturally more empathetic, while others are trained to be over time. Whatever the case, you can become more empathetic through certain action steps. We will go over those here.

Challenge Yourself

Many times, people become non-empathetic because they don't remember, or ever knew, what it was like to experience discomfort. If you challenge yourself by going out of your comfort zone, you will start understanding what it's like to be in an uncomfortable setting, like so many people are. It makes you less soft.

To challenge yourself, you can do something out of the ordinary every day, like going to a new restaurant or trying an activity you've never done before. You can take courses to increase your skillset, like learning a new language, taking an art class, or signing up for training at a local college. You can also do something more daring, like skydiving or bungee-jumping if you are willing to.

Doing things to get you out of your comfort zone will humble you, and humility is one of the main enablers of empathy.

Get Out of Your Usual Environment

Do you believe that the rest of the world thinks just like you do? Are you unaware of the many cultures that exist out there? If so, it is time for you to get out of your familiar environment. You don't have to travel abroad even though that is an option. Just go somewhere you have never been before, even if that place is just a few towns over. Being in a different setting will give you a new perspective you've never had before. By doing this, you will develop a greater appreciation for other people. You will soon realize that not everyone lives and thinks like you, and this can be very enlightening. You will soon learn that another person will view the world from a different lens. This realization is also important for empathy to occur.

Get Feedback

Ask for feedback from people who know you well, like friends, family, or colleagues. Have them give you their opinions on the various skills you possess, like listening, asking questions, body language, facial expression, and other communication factors. Ask for feedback frequently so you stay sharp.

Explore the Heart, Not Just the Head

A technique that many medical schools use to increase empathy in their future doctors is to have them read literature that explores emotions and personal relationships. This strategy makes people realize that other people have specific emotions and feelings during certain situations, and they may be vastly different from your own. This is a simple trick you can start using, especially if you love to read. Another option is watching emotional movies or TV shows.

Walk in Other People's Shoes

We don't mean this literally, but you can ask other people what it is like to live in their current situation. What moods are they going through and why? What is the underlying reason behind this and are their specific triggers? Slowly but surely, this technique will teach you about other people's experiences and how they perceived similar experiences as you went through. Once you start walking to people about how they felt during certain moments that you also went through, you begin learning how the viewpoints of some people are drastically different than yours. You will begin understanding that not everyone thinks or reacts like you and they're not necessarily wrong in doing that.

. . .

Examine Your Biases

We all have biases that prevent us from being fully empathetic. Biases are judgments we are making towards a person without having much knowledge of the situation. For example, if we see someone who is overweight, we might assume they are lazy and don't take care of themselves. We don't take into account that there could be certain factors beyond their control. It is important to examine your biases and assess how they are causing you to jump to conclusions. If you don't think you have any biases, think again. Sometimes, they become so ingrained in us that we don't realize they are there.

Cultivate Your Sense of Curiosity

We have already described this as an essential coaching skill and it is a great way to develop empathy. What can you learn from a new employee who comes into your office? What can you learn from your child? What can you learn from your client? Curious people ask a lot of questions and follow up questions too until they arrive at an answer. You will do this with your clients too, which will naturally boost your empathy. Oh, and asking good questions is the final action step we are going to mention towards improving empathy.

7

LEADERSHIP DEVELOPMENT COACH

"Leadership is about making others better as a result of your presence and making sure that impact lasts in your absence."

— SHERYL SANBERG, COO OF FACEBOOK

A leader is anyone who has the responsibility of managing a group. There can be many different variations of leaders. Most people think of CEOs, high-level executives, or business-owners as leaders. Managers and supervisors can also be placed in this category. A leader can be a person who is heading up a particular group project. Heads of households, like parents or guardians, can be considered leaders, as well.

Being a leader is not so much about having a title, but how you conduct yourself. Leaders are those who command attention and respect through words and actions. Leaders will often rise to the top of any situation and will often step forward to accept challenges, while others step back. A leader is able to inspire others to be their best selves. Finally, they are the ones people look to for guidance, whether they are in a leadership role or not. Their presence is attractive to people.

While true leaders don't always have to be in an official role, most of them naturally shift towards these positions because of how they carry themselves. In times of crisis, people look towards a strong leader. This is why they must be taken care of too.

"People who are truly strong lift others up. People who are truly powerful bring others together."

— MICHELLE OBAMA

Leadership

LEADERSHIP DEVELOPMENT COACHING

Who is guiding these leaders to become the best versions of themselves? Oftentimes, it is a leadership development coach, which is a sector of business coaching that we will discuss here. Having good leaders is essential in our society, but too many of them take the wrong approach when it comes to actual leadership. After a while, the people they are leading can start to lose faith and stop following directions. The members of a group may even start blaming their leader for failures they have personally encountered.

Leadership development coaches are there to guide leadership clients in developing their essential qualities. These types of coaches can help leaders understand their shortcomings in order to correct them. The relationship is a collaborative effort to achieve a set goal. The overall objective is to transform the quality of a leader's work and personal life.

Leadership development coaching:

- Improves the skills and knowledge of their clients.
- Provides a foundation for better work-life balance.
- Works to develop higher emotional intelligence.
- Helps leaders at the interpersonal and organizational levels.

Leadership development coaching is many things, but here's what it's not:

- Technical guidance
- Consulting
- Career counseling
- Job training

It is simply a partnership that helps leaders accomplish short-term and long-term organizational goals.

BENEFITS OF LEADERSHIP DEVELOPMENT COACHING

Leadership development has some interesting benefits to consider.

Flow-on Effect

This type of coaching leads to effective leaders and healthier organizations. As leaders are able to improve their skills, the positive benefits will spread across the entire organization.

Leaders in any sector are the ones who set the tone for whatever environment they are in. So, if they can show strength through their emotions, it will have an impact on everyone around them. Senior leaders who are exposed to leadership development coaching develop a flow-on effect, which creates a new coaching culture within an organization.

Leaders learn new skills through an effective coaching process and pass them on to those who follow them. This results in improved performance, productivity, and better outcomes. Creating a coaching environment leads to space where people will be empathetic, understanding, patient, and helpful to one another just like any coach would be.

Personalized Attention

As many more organizations are looking to operate at peak performance, coaching is becoming a viable option to get them there. Many businesses go the route of seminars, workshops, and other training programs. However, these options are very generalized with the same information for all groups. Coaching is much more targeted and tailored towards a particular person or organization's needs. This personal attention is what makes the field of coaching so attractive.

Coaches use their training and skills to analyze each individual and help them explore their full potential. The process of coaching challenges clients in a way they've never been before and forces them out of their comfort zone. They realize that many of the beliefs they had their whole lives are not as real as they once thought. After working with a coach, business clients will begin welcoming change, which is needed for growth.

Personalized attention

SKILLS NEEDED FOR LEADERSHIP DEVELOPMENT COACHING

Just like any other type of coaching, leadership development coaching requires a proper skill set. You cannot become a hirable coach without these attributes. Let's go over some of them.

Communication Skills

This is pretty much a given, but in order to be a great coach, you need to be a great communicator. This does just not mean you are good at talking. It encompasses all aspects of communications. You will get a wide variety of clients throughout your career who come from different backgrounds, cultures, and socioeconomic statuses. Some individuals will be extroverts, while others will be introverts. You will need to learn how to communicate well with all of them.

As a coach, you must encourage people to tell their side of the story and then listen actively to what they say. You need to be able to pick up on clues and ask good follow up questions, summarize, and reflect on what they said. Poor communication will result in a lot of misunderstandings. Make sure the messages going both ways are as crisp and clear as possible.

Always keep in mind that your tone, body language, and attitude matter, as well. It's what just what you say, but how you say it, and when you say it. You will have many challenging clients who will test your patience. You must not lose your cool. Take any criticism and resistance in a positive way by always responding with gentleness. Using proper communication methods will help ease your client's tension. Think of yourself as a leader during a coaching session and act as a leader would.

Influencing and Negotiation Skills

The best leadership development coaches do not command authority. They do not boss people around or control them in any way. Instead, they inspire and encourage others. Just like any coach and client relationship, it is a collaboration between two people trying to learn more about the coachee.

Great leaders know that influence matters much more than power. They know how to negotiate a deal so it's not all one-sided, but a win-win for all who are involved. As a leadership development coach, you must practice what you preach. Before you can help your clients develop their leadership skills, you must have them yourself.

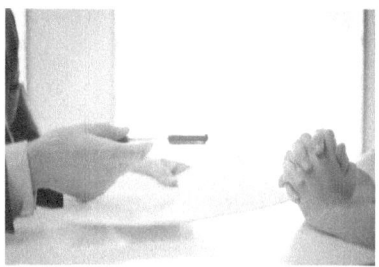

Negotiating

Conflict Management Skills

There are some people in this world who are always ready for conflict and will create it whenever they can. Sometimes, conflict just arises out of nowhere. As a coach, you will have clients like this and they will be difficult to manage. Some of them will be short-tempered while others will be in situations that will make them act this way. Some clients will have no hope and resist the coaching process heavily. Finally, some of your clients will blame you for their failures. There is the potential for many different conflicts to arise so you must be able to manage it as a coach.

As a leadership development coach, you will have two main advantages in regards to conflict management skills:

- It will help in your coaching process.
- You will set a great example for your client. They will learn to manage and resolve conflicts by taking inspiration from you.

By displaying conflict management skills, your client will become a better leader.

Change Management Skills

A coaching session will never be predictable and you never know when you will need to change things up. You may have had a strong plan going in, but that can change at the drop of a hat. As you proceed with the coaching sessions with your clients, you will experience many changes.

In addition, there will be many difficult situations that you will face, and there is a possibility that you will not get clients right away. You need to have change management skills in order to deal with unpredictable situations.

Questioning and Listening Skills

Questioning and listening are the best ways to understand the situation your client is currently in. We have already gone over asking appropriate questions and listening skills but just wanted to reiterate their importance here. Never be in a rush to get to the next question.

. . .

Analyzing Skills

Once you have identified the points of pain for a client, the next step is to analyze them thoroughly. The following are some questions you can ask:

- What is the cause of the pain?
- What options are available for you?
- What potential alternatives exist?
- What strengths and weaknesses do you possess?
- What should you focus on to transform into the leader you want to be?

Analyze the current situation thoroughly while also having the end goal in mind.

PRINCIPLES OF LEADERSHIP DEVELOPMENT COACHING

Along with the coaching skills, there are specific principles involved in leadership development coaching that you must also be aware of. These principles will guide your coaching process if you incorporate them into your practice.

Align With the Coachee's Agenda

The cardinal rule of coaching is that it must be client-focused and never about you as the coach. Your goal is to do what's best for your client, so you must put your ego aside and become humble. Therefore, never tell the coachee what they should be focused on or what needs to be the priority in their lives. They need to figure this out on their own. You can guide them as needed, but do not impose your will in any way on them.

A leadership development coach simply helps their client discover the answers they already have within them.

Collaborate

The leadership development coach should only act as a collaborator in assisting their clients, but the coachee has the ultimate say. In fact, a coach should not really sway their decision one way or another. They can just help facilitate the transition.

Advocate Self-Awareness

Self-awareness means having a conscious knowledge of one's current status, characters, desires, feelings, and motives. A good leader should always be self-aware of their particular strengths and weaknesses. Exhibit a sense of self-awareness within yourself and your client will foster something similar within themselves. Once again, you can lead by example.

Always model the leadership qualities that you try to instill in your clients. Practice what you preach and your clients will have greater faith in knowing what you are talking about.

WHY HIRE A LEADERSHIP DEVELOPMENT COACH

If you are not already convinced about the benefits of leadership development coaching or the coaching practice in general, then continue reading to fully recognize why someone would hire a coach in this regard. If you want to explain to potential clients why they should hire you, the following reasons are a great start.

Empowerment

Leadership development coaches can empower their clients to become powerful leaders and do exceptional work. Through the use of several coaching tools and techniques, you can help a client discover their full potential. You can get them to think in a way they never have before. The relationship a client has with their coach will help them achieve some much-needed transformation to vastly change their circumstances.

Fresh Insight

Leaders can gain some fresh perspective from their coach. During times of great stress and feeling overwhelmed a client may not be able to see things clearly. The coach can help them sit back and reflect on their situation. The coach can analyze what is happening through a different lens and find deeper problems. From here, the coach can build a plan to tackle similar problems in the future.

Free Thinking

Coaches will allow free-thinking in their clients. Many people are in structured environments where they must think a certain way or think very quickly to get the job done. During a coaching session, the client actually has some time to reflect. They can also consider different thought patterns and views. Free thinking encourages flexible leadership, which is important for decision-making.

Enhanced Performance

The leadership development coaching process makes a huge difference in someone's attitude and abilities. Coaches help their clients learn and put in place new techniques. These strategies are tailored around clients' weaknesses and help them avoid self-defeating words, like "but," "maybe," or "yet." A leadership development coach will help transform the personality of a leader to make them stronger in their field. The transformation alone is worth the investment in coaching.

BUSINESS/LIFE BALANCE

Now that we have covered business coaching in great detail, we will go over some ways a coach can help their clients set up a work/life balance. Or in our case, business/life balance. This is something that will become part of your skillset as a coach. The purpose of running a business is to have autonomy so you have some freedom to run your life. If you are working all the time, that reason becomes moot.

Whether you are a small business owner or run a large corporation, a big chunk of your life will be dedicated to your business. The hours are long and the rewards are few at the very beginning. While being a business owner does ask a lot of someone, you must never lose sight of the fact that you have a personal life.

As a business coach, you will be running your own business too, so maintaining work/life balance is important for you, as well. This is another opportunity for you to be an example for your client. Once you develop the skills to maintain balance in your life, you can impart your knowledge to your client. As always, your goal will be to guide them towards their own path. We will no go over some ways to create and sustain a balance between business and personal life.

Get Help

Business owners, especially when they are new, have a tendency to take on a lot of responsibility on their own. Normally, this is the work of multiple people being done by one individual. If you are going to maintain work/life balance, you cannot expect to do it all on your own and not work 24/7.

Consider hiring people to help you with certain tasks and projects. As a business coach, you can help your client figure out what areas of their business can be done by other people so they have the time to focus on more important items that require more of their attention. If you don't want to hire full-time employees, you can hire independent contractors.

Set a Schedule

If you want to get everything done, you must set a schedule that will structure your day into specific blocks. For example, you can block off specific hours of the days for certain business-related items while also setting aside time blocks for fun and relaxation. Once you set up your schedule, stick to the times as much as possible.

As a business coach, you can assist your client in creating a proper schedule that will work well for their needs. When the day is structured and you have a plan, it is much easier to find time to do the things you want to do.

Prioritize

To balance your life properly, you need to prioritize what is important to you. Always put your most important tasks first and get them over with. That way, if you need to push anything back, it will be your less urgent items on the list. When you are setting your priorities, make self-care one of them. Block off time for self-care and stick to these times as much as possible.

Take Breaks

You cannot run around all day at work without sitting down or taking a break. You will burn out and be unable to function in other areas of your life. Carve out time every day whether you are at work or home.

Get a Hobby

When you run a business of any kind, it is nearly impossible to completely separate your business life from your personal life. This is just the nature of the entrepreneur beast. To help combat this, find a hobby that is completely separate from work and something you will never mix in with your business. Once you have your hobby, set aside time for it every week.

Take Time Off

When you are running your own business, we know it can seem impossible to just take time off. After all, when you are not open, you are not making money. If you are working seven days a week, spending some quality time to yourself at the end of every day is not enough. You need more time than this. Try to take at least one day off in a week to get away from your business. As a coach, you can help your client explore which day of the week is generally the slowest on average and encourage the client to take that particular day off every week. It's worth a shot to get some relaxation.

Set Boundaries

Since you cannot separate your business life and personal life completely, you can at least set some boundaries. When you are doing stuff for your business, try to keep your personal life out of it. When you are at home, try to avoid bringing your business issues into it. You can also make rules that you will not do any business-related activities after a certain time. Whatever you can do to maintain a boundary, do it.

Find Your Productivity

Get the most out of your workday by finding your productivity. The more productive you are, the more tasks you will get done within a specific time period which means more of your personal time will remain your personal time.

Stay Connected

A major part of having a personal life is staying connected with other people. Healthy relationships that are not work-related are essential for maintaining balance. Stay involved with your friends, make time to spend with them, be an active member of your community, and spend whatever time you can away from the demands of your business.

As you can see, the strategies we covered throughout this book will help to create a positive work/life balance. Be that example for your clients and improve your work/life balance.

CONCLUSION

We had a great time writing this book, *Who Wants to Be a Superhero If You Can be a Business Coach?* All of us at Elvin Coaches want to thank you for taking the time to read it. We hope that you are as excited about learning business coaching as we are talking about it. Coaching is a powerful industry that can change people's lives in an instant. In fact, it has been for many decades now and all of us have seen this happen personally.

Business coaching is a major sector of the larger life coaching industry where the focus is to help clients build their business no matter what state they are in. Whether someone is just thinking about transitioning into the business world, is actively opening up their first business, or has been successful in business for years, they can all benefit heavily from a business coach.

Business coaching utilizes effective techniques, the most common ones being asking appropriate questions and listening with intent. These methods help guide business clients to find the best solutions to their problems. Like any other type of life coach, a business coach will never tell a client what to do but will help them explore the answers that are already inside of them. This is where the best solutions are found. When someone is able to figure things out on their own, it is a big boost to their self-confidence. Coaching works from the assumption that all people are capable of solving their problems, they just need some direction along the way.

After reading this book, we anticipate that you have a thorough understanding of what business coaching is, what benefits it can have for entrepreneurs, and the steps you can take to become one yourself if you desire to do so. Our hope is that you gained an interest in this field and will decide to partake in it in the future. We love the coaching industry and want as many talented people to join our profession.

In this book, we also covered the various sunsets of business coaching, like leadership development coaching and time management coaching. If you can find a good specialty that interests you within the business coaching field, you will be able to work with a niche market and provide in-depth help towards a targeted group.

Marketing is something you cannot forget about, whether you are the coach or the client. This means that you must take advantage of effective marketing strategies in your coaching business and guide your clients in proper advertising methods for their own venture, whatever it may be. No matter how good a product, service, or idea is, no one will know it exists if the marketing is not done properly. The advertising and marketing industries are changing and innovating constantly. Staying up to date on the newest trends is essential for optimal success.

Despite what area of business coaching you get into, many of the same principles for success will apply. Of course, each sector will have their own unique methods as well. Overall, before you get into business coaching on your own, fully understand the role you will play and the strategies you need to help your clients to the best of your ability. It is advisable to hire a business coach of your own to help make the transition smooth. The focus of any coaching session is the client that needs help. A coach should use these opportunities to provide as much value to their coachee as possible, and not worry about their ego or reputation. A reputation will be built once the clients start spreading the word about your coaching strategies. Give them something good to talk about.

Once you become a business coach and attract multiple clients, you will be your own boss and will benefit from the freedom of being an entrepreneur. Of course, the classic joke here is that an entrepreneur will work eighty hours a week for themselves to avoid working forty hours a week for someone else. There is definitely an element of truth to this statement. However, working for yourself still gives you a sense of freedom despite how many hours you may be working.

Along with guiding their clients towards successful business practices, coaches will also help their clients develop a work/life balance. Business owners will put in many hours and it is impossible to completely separate work issues from personal matters. At some point, one area will bleed into the other and vice versa. Of course, this does not mean that certain practices cannot be put in place to limit the crossover between business and home life. With the amount of stress owning a business can create, it is essential to break away regularly to decompress and re-energize.

Business coaching is a dynamic field and all of us at Elvin Coaches are excited that you got a taste of what the coaching industry is all about. We say taste because the field encompasses so much, and you must experience it first hand to understand what it entails.

If you are excited about what you've read so far and want to experience business coaching first hand, do not wait any longer. Do your research about coaches in your area and try out a few sessions. We expect that you are involved, or plan to be involved, in some type of business. After experiencing the benefits of coaching, you can work on becoming a business coach yourself, if that is your goal. The prospects are great and the industry, as a whole, is growing exponentially. As more people realize the value of coaching, it will continue to grow and prosper. We are confident that once you start participating in the coaching practice, both as a client and coach, you will never look back.

Finally, we want as many people as possible to learn about the field of business coaching. If you found the information to be valuable, a positive review would be greatly appreciated so more people can learn about this book and benefit from it. Thank you again for taking the time to read it.

Freedom

PLEASE LEAVE A REVIEW

Did you enjoy the book??

Reviews are the life blood of an author. If you can please take a few minutes to leave a review.

Even a short review helps, like "Great book!".

Just for you!

A FREE GIFT TO OUR READERS

Scan the QR code to subscribe or follow the link
https://elvinlifecoaches.activehosted.com/f/3

You're going to receive the

Wheel of Life Coaching Technique

and other goodies

REFERENCES

18 Examples of Bad Coaching Habits. (2016, May 10). Center for Executive Coaching. https://www.centerforexecutivecoaching.com/articles/bad-coaching-habits/

Achieving Work-Life Balance as a Small Business Owner. (2020, February 4). Ama La Vida. https://alvcoaching.com/work-life-balance-small-business-owner/

Blackbyrn, Sai. "Become An Amazing Leadership Development Coach In 2020 - .Coach." ..*Coach*, .Coach Blog, 20 June 2020, sai.coach/blog/leadership-development-coach-2020/. Accessed 8 Oct. 2020.

Blackbyrn, Sai. "How To Become The Best Marketing Coach In 2020 - .Coach." ..*Coach*, .Coach Blog, 3 Mar. 2020, sai.coach/blog/marketing-coach-2020/. Accessed 9 Oct. 2020.

Bluepoint Leadership Development. "The Three Core Coaching Skills." *YouTube*, 27 Aug. 2013, www.youtube.com/watch?v=bYZZQigqZQs. Accessed 6 Oct. 2020.

Boolkah, P. (2017). What Does A Business Coach Do? | The Benefits Of Coaching And Mentoring For Business Owners [YouTube Video]. In *YouTube*. https://www.youtube.com/watch?v=BqLhT8hJpuQ

Breakingpic. (n.d.). *Green Note Card and Four Scrabble Tiles on Gray Surface*. Retrieved October 8, 2020, from https://www.pexels.com/photo/postit-scrabble-to-do-todo-3299/

Burrows, Kate. "Coaching Skills | Ultimate Guide | Coaching Techniques." *Making Business Matter*, 3 Apr. 2018, www.makingbusinessmatter.co.uk/coaching-skills-ultimate-guide/#10. Accessed 9 Oct. 2020.

Cabello, A. (n.d.). *Man Blindfolded*. Retrieved October 9, 2020, from https://www.pexels.com/photo/man-blindfolded-1278620/

Christian, L. (2019, July 9). *What is a Business Coach (and Are They Effective in 2020)?* SoulSalt. https://soulsalt.com/what-is-a-business-coach/

Chuangch, A. (n.d.). *Black Analog Alarm Clock at 7:01*. Retrieved October 6, 2020, from https://www.pexels.com/photo/accurate-alarm-alarm-clock-analogue-359989/

Duczeminski, Matt. "5 Reasons to Embrace Vulnerability." *Lifehack*, 19 June 2015, www.lifehack.org/273700/5-reasons-embrace-vulnerability. Accessed 9 Oct. 2020.

Fauxels. (n.d.-b). *Photo of People Near Wooden Table*. Retrieved October 6, 2020, from https://www.pexels.com/photo/photo-of-people-near-wooden-table-3184418/

Fewtrell, B. (2019, July 11). *Build & Grow your Business with MaxMyProfit*. MaxMyProfit. https://maxmyprofit.com.au/blog/7-step-guide-to-becoming-a-business-coach/

Foo, S. (2020, May 4). *Blogging As Your Marketing Tool: How It Works & Why To Start*. SpeechSilver. https://speechsilver.com/blogging-as-your-marketing-tool/

Forbes Coaches Council. (2018, January 25). *Council Post: 15 Effective Ways To Establish Credibility As A Business Coach*. Forbes. https://www.forbes.com/sites/forbescoachescouncil/2018/01/25/15-effective-ways-to-establish-credibility-as-a-business-coach/#3689c73ad23b

Guthrie, G. (2018, October 24). *8 Essential Questioning Techniques You Need to Know*. Typetalk. https://www.typetalk.com/blog/the-8-essential-questioning-techniques-you-need-to-know/

Pixabay. (n.d.-h). *Group of People Holding Arms*. Retrieved October 8, 2020, from https://www.pexels.com/photo/ground-group-growth-hands-461049/

Juhaszimrus, S. (n.d.). *123 Let's Go Imaginary Text*. Retrieved October 8, 2020, from https://www.pexels.com/photo/123-lets-go-imaginary-text-704767/

Kaboompics.com. (n.d.). *Customers & Users/Color Wheel*. Retrieved October 8, 2020, from https://www.pexels.com/photo/customers-users-color-wheel-6231/

Komar, Marlen. "7 Ways To Let Yourself Become More Vulnerable." *Bustle*, 28 Mar. 2016, www.bustle.com/articles/150219-7-ways-to-let-yourself-become-more-vulnerable. Accessed 9 Oct. 2020.

Lui, E. (n.d.). *Signboard with Time is Precious title on black background*. Retrieved October 8, 2020, from https://www.pexels.com/photo/signboard-with-time-is-precious-title-on-black-background-4151043/

Magni, O. (n.d.). *Person Resting Their Hand on Table*. Retrieved October 8, 2020, from https://www.pexels.com/photo/person-resting-their-hand-on-table-2058147/

Mazumder, A. (n.d.). *Person Holding a Green Plant*. Retrieved October 8, 2020, from https://www.pexels.com/photo/person-holding-a-green-plant-1072824/

McCarthy, Dan. "70 Coaching Questions for Managers Using the GROW Model." *The Balance Careers*, 19 Nov. 2019, www.thebalancecareers.com/coaching-questions-for-managers-2275913. Accessed 9 Oct. 2020.

Miller, Dan. "7 Reasons I Love Being a Coach." *Official Site Dan Miller*, 30 June 2015, www.48days.com/7-reasons-i-love-being-a-coach/. Accessed 9 Oct. 2020.

Mind Tools Content Team. (2009b). *How Can I Stop Procrastinating?Overcoming the Habit of Delaying Important Tasks*. Mindtools.Com. https://www.mindtools.com/pages/article/newHTE_96.htm

Mindvalley. (n.d.-b). *Ultimate Guide To Becoming a Business Coach*. Evercoach - By Mindvalley. Retrieved October 2, 2020, from https://www.evercoach.com/ultimate-guide-to-becoming-a-business-coach

Newlands, M. (2015, January 9). *10 Simple Steps to Improve Productivity*. Inc.Com. https://www.inc.com/murray-newlands/10-simple-steps-to-improve-productivity.html

Pixabay. (n.d.-l). *Questions Answers Signage*. Retrieved October 8, 2020, from https://www.pexels.com/photo/questions-answers-signage-208494/

Pixabay. (n.d.-l). *Red and Yellow Hatchback Axa Crash Tests*. Retrieved October 8, 2020, from https://www.pexels.com/photo/red-and-yellow-hatchback-axa-crash-tests-163016/

Roseclay, D. (n.d.). *Brown Framed Eyeglasses*. Retrieved October 9, 2020, from https://www.pexels.com/photo/brown-framed-eyeglasses-905163/

Scott, S. J. (2016, January 19). *How to Form a New Habit (in 8 Easy Steps)*. Develop Good Habits. https://www.developgoodhabits.com/how-to-form-a-habit-in-8-easy-steps/

Sobel, A. (2016). *Eight Ways to Improve Your Empathy*. Andrewsobel.Com. https://andrewsobel.com/eight-ways-to-improve-your-empathy/

Spiske, M. (n.d.). Retrieved October 8, 2020, from https://www.pexels.com/photo/crowd-reflection-color-toy-1679618/

Stavrinos, S. (n.d.). *Monochrome Photography of People Shaking Hands*. Retrieved October 6, 2020, from https://www.pexels.com/photo/monochrome-photography-of-people-shaking-hands-814544/

Tang, Cham. "The 4 Marketing Fundamentals." *Authentic Education*, 2 Feb. 2018, www.authentic.com.au/blog/marketing/4-marketing-fundamentals/. Accessed 9 Oct. 2020.

Thanyakij, B. (n.d.). *Person Writing on White Paper*. Retrieved October 8, 2020, from https://www.pexels.com/photo/person-writing-on-white-paper-3815585/

Timely Blog. "5 Essential Time Management Techniques – Timely Blog." *Memory*, 27 Aug. 2020, memory.ai/timely-blog/time-management-techniques. Accessed 9 Oct. 2020.

Wade, Francis. "How to Make a Difference as a Time Management Coach." *Lifehack*, 2 May 2012, www.lifehack.org/articles/productivity/how-to-make-a-difference-as-a-time-management-coach.html. Accessed 9 Oct. 2020.

Winkler, M. (n.d.-b). *Green Typewriter on Brown Wooden Table*. Retrieved October 6, 2020, from https://www.pexels.com/photo/green-typewriter-on-brown-wooden-table-4052198/

www.ingramcontent.com/pod-product-compliance
Lightning Source LLC
Chambersburg PA
CBHW021429080526
44588CB00009B/467